THE AVENGERS
AND
PHILOSOPHY

The Blackwell Philosophy and Pop Culture Series
Series Editor: William Irwin

South Park and Philosophy
Edited by Robert Arp

Metallica and Philosophy
Edited by William Irwin

Family Guy and Philosophy
Edited by J. Jeremy Wisnewski

The Daily Show and Philosophy
Edited by Jason Holt

Lost and Philosophy
Edited by Sharon Kaye

24 and Philosophy
*Edited by Jennifer Hart Weed,
Richard Davis, and Ronald Weed*

Battlestar Galactica and Philosophy
Edited by Jason T. Eberl

The Office and Philosophy
Edited by J. Jeremy Wisnewski

Batman and Philosophy
Edited by Mark D. White and Robert Arp

House and Philosophy
Edited by Henry Jacoby

Watchmen and Philosophy
Edited by Mark D. White

X-Men and Philosophy
*Edited by Rebecca Housel and
J. Jeremy Wisnewski*

Terminator and Philosophy
*Edited by Richard Brown and
Kevin Decker*

Heroes and Philosophy
Edited by David Kyle Johnson

Twilight and Philosophy
*Edited by Rebecca Housel and
J. Jeremy Wisnewski*

Final Fantasy and Philosophy
*Edited by Jason P. Blahuta and
Michel S. Beaulieu*

Alice in Wonderland and Philosophy
Edited by Richard Brian Davis

Iron Man and Philosophy
Edited by Mark D. White

True Blood and Philosophy
*Edited by George Dunn and
Rebecca Housel*

Mad Men and Philosophy
*Edited by James South and
Rod Carveth*

30 Rock and Philosophy
Edited by J. Jeremy Wisnewski

The Ultimate Harry Potter
and Philosophy
Edited by Gregory Bassham

The Ultimate Lost and Philosophy
Edited by Sharon Kaye

Green Lantern and Philosophy
*Edited by Jane Dryden and Mark
D. White*

The Girl with the Dragon Tattoo
and Philosophy
Edited by Eric Bronson

Arrested Development and Philosophy
*Edited by Kristopher Phillips
and J. Jeremy Wisnewski*

Inception and Philosophy
Edited by David Johnson

The Big Lebowski and Philosophy
Edited by Peter S. Fosl

Spider-Man and Philosophy
Edited by Jonathan Sanford

The Big Bang Theory and
Philosophy
Edited by Dean Kowalski

The Hunger Games and Philosophy
*Edited by George Dunn and
Nicolas Michaud*

Game of Thrones and Philosophy
Edited by Henry Jacoby

THE AVENGERS
AND
PHILOSOPHY

EARTH'S MIGHTIEST THINKERS

Edited by Mark D. White

WILEY

John Wiley & Sons, Inc.

Published by John Wiley & Sons, Inc., Hoboken, New Jersey
Published simultaneously in Canada

Chapter opener design by Forty-five Degree Design LLC

For general information about our other products and services, please contact our Customer Care Department within the United States at (800) 762-2974, outside the United States at (317) 572-3993 or fax (317) 572-4002.

Wiley also publishes its books in a variety of electronic formats and by print-on-demand. Some content that appears in standard print versions of this book may not be available in other formats. For more information about Wiley products, visit us at www.wiley.com.

The Avengers and philosophy : Earth's mightiest thinkers / edited by Mark D. White.
    pages   cm. — (The Blackwell philosophy and pop culture series ; 46)
    Includes bibliographical references and index.
    ISBN 978-1-118-07457-2 (paper); ISBN 978-1-118-22253-9 (ebk);
    ISBN 978-1-118-23645-1 (ebk); ISBN 978-1-118-26138-5 (ebk)
        1. Avengers (Fictitious characters) 2. Comic books, strips, etc.—Moral and ethi-cal aspects. 3. Superheroes in literature. 4. Superhero films—History and criticism. 5. Philosophy in literature. 6. Philosophy in motion pictures. I. White, Mark D., 1971- editor of compilation.
    PN6728.A9A93   2012
    791.43'652—dc23

                                                                            2011043329

10 9 8 7 6 5 4 3 2 1

CONTENTS

INTRODUCTION: EARTH'S MIGHTIEST PHILOSOPHERS

If you like superheroes—and you wouldn't be reading this book if you didn't—you *love* superhero teams, and the Avengers are the preeminent team in the Marvel Universe. The best thing about the Avengers is that not only do you get to see all your favorite heroes banding together to defeat formidable threats against incredible odds, but you also get to see them interact both as superheroes *and* as people. Whether they're cooped up in Avengers Mansion or exploring the deepest realms of space, you get to see how they work together and play together, both when they get along and when they don't. That's what we love about the Avengers, whether in the comics, the animated series, or the feature film—it's equal parts superhero epic and soap opera.

Just as the Avengers assemble to confront threats no single hero can handle himself or herself, the contributors to *The Avengers and Philosophy* assembled to discuss a range of topics so broad that no single philosopher could possibly handle it all.

Have you ever wondered how the "big three" Avengers—Captain America, Iron Man, and Thor—compare in terms of their moral philosophies? Has the Kree-Skrull War ever made you consider the ethics of war itself? What about the Avengers' peculiar tendency to welcome former criminals into their ranks, such as Hawkeye, Quicksilver, and the Scarlet Witch? We didn't forget to ask questions about the great Avengers villains: Can Kang actually go back in time to kill himself? Do we actually admire Norman Osborn and his Dark Avengers? And finally, speaking of soap opera, can the Scarlet Witch and the Vision truly love each other?

No matter what Avengers lineup you prefer, or which Avenger is your favorite, there's a chapter in *The Avengers and Philosophy* for you. (Why no Squirrel Girl, you ask? Wait for volume two—it's *all* her.) So until Avengers Academy opens a branch near you, this book is the best way to learn from Earth's Mightiest Philosophers—until we get our own movie, that is!

■ ■ ■

I would like to thank Bill Irwin for his constant support, encouragement, and hard work on this book and the Blackwell Philosophy and Pop Culture series as a whole; Connie Santisteban at Wiley, who saw this book through from beginning to end; and my fellow contributors, who came through with insights into philosophy and the Avengers I would never have imagined. I also want to give special thanks to Christine Hanefalk, who was incredibly supportive, especially in the stressful final weeks of this project. Finally, I would like to thank all the creators who have made the Avengers shine for half a century, starting with Stan Lee and Jack Kirby, through Kurt Busiek and George Pérez, and all the way up to Brian Michael Bendis, and Joss Whedon for bringing Earth's Mightiest Heroes to life on the silver screen.

PART ONE

WHAT WOULD AN AVENGER DO?

SUPERHUMAN ETHICS CLASS WITH THE AVENGERS PRIME

Mark D. White

At Avengers Academy, where veterans like Hank Pym and Tigra teach younger heroes in the ways of Avengerdom, one of the required courses is Superhuman Ethics Class. In this class, superpupils are presented with ethical dilemmas that crop up in the day-to-day "routine" of an Avenger, and then they are asked how they would handle them and why. We may recoil at the thought of Hank Pym teaching this class—the poster child for "Do what I say, not as I've done myself time and time again"— but such a class is essential to teach young heroes how to exercise the great responsibility that comes with great power.[1]

If you ask me, the most obvious teachers for Superhuman Ethics Class would be Captain America, Iron Man, and Thor, who were christened the "Avengers Prime" in a recent miniseries.[2] I'm not claiming that these three are necessarily the most ethical Avengers, but they do serve as examples of the three most popular systems of ethics: utilitarianism, deontology, and virtue ethics. While each of these three classic heroes exemplifies his particular moral compass in his solo adventures, it is through their interactions—especially their conflicts—within the Avengers that they best illustrate their different ethical approaches. Let's start with Iron Man because his ethical framework is in many ways the simplest, and also because he sets the stage for introducing the other two in contrast.

The Utilitarian Iron Man

Tony Stark has long been an important figure in the Marvel Universe, but starting with the "Civil War" event in 2006, he became central to it. As soon as he realized that passage of the Superhuman Registration Act, a law requiring all superheroes to register and reveal their identities to the government, was inevitable, he got in front of it and made sure it was implemented *his* way. When Captain America started a superhero resistance against the law, Iron Man led the pro-registration forces against him, and after the war ended with Cap's surrender, Tony was granted control of S.H.I.E.L.D. and the Avengers. During that tenure, he had to deal with the death of Captain America (Steve Rogers) and the anointment of his successor (Bucky Barnes), the destruction of New York City by the same Hulk he had helped to exile to space years before, and a full-scale secret invasion by the Skrulls. The Skrull debacle led to the downfall of Tony Stark, the rise of Norman Osborn, and Tony's self-lobotomization to ensure that Osborn would not get the superhero registration information stored in his brain. Osborn's "Dark Reign" ended with the Siege of Asgard after Tony (with most of his mind restored), Steve Rogers (back from the dead), and Thor (now a proud Oklahoman) reunited to lead the assorted Avengers teams against him.[3]

Many people, in both the Marvel Universe and the real world, found Tony's decisions and actions during this period despicable, especially during the Civil War, when he enlisted the Thunderbolts, a team of known supervillains and psychopaths, to round up unregistered heroes, and helped build a prison in the Negative Zone to hold them. It's hard to doubt Tony's sincere motivation to make things better, though. And rarely can things be made better without breaking some rules or creating some negative consequences.

The issues of broken rules and negative consequences are familiar to moral philosophers because they also apply to *utilitarianism*, Tony Stark's basic ethical system. Utilitarianism judges actions by the goodness (or "utility") of their consequences. An action that creates more good than bad in the world is ethical, and the action that creates most good compared to bad is the most ethical (or required). The philosopher credited with introducing utilitarianism, Jeremy Bentham (1748–1832), equated "good" with pleasure and "bad" with pain. Other utilitarians have also proposed happiness, well-being, or preference satisfaction as ways to think of utility.[4] However utility or goodness is measured, utilitarianism is based on the common-sense notion that outcomes matter. Furthermore, everyone's utility is equally important. This means that goodness can be added up to arrive at a sum total for each action, which can be used for comparisons of alternatives or maximization to arrive at the morally best plan of action.[5]

While the concept of utilitarianism is very simple, in practice it can become very complicated because measuring the utility of various options is incredibly difficult. In order to evaluate and compare the goodness of different courses of action, a person must trace out all the effects of each choice. Of course, Tony Stark regards himself as a futurist, uniquely able to see the results of any event. After defeating the Crimson Dynamo by stopping his heart and then immediately reviving him, Cap dresses Tony down, saying, "You could have stopped the situation without stopping the man's heart. I can think of at least four—" but Tony interrupts with, "And I can think of seven. But this one was the most expedient."[6] Even on this relatively small scale, however, the chain of events flowing from that choice can be hard to predict, especially when other people and random events intervene. (For instance, the Dynamo may have had a heart condition that prevented Tony from restarting it.)

When it comes to monumental decisions like exiling the Hulk or supporting superhero registration, the countless and complex ramifications are impossible to know and therefore impossible to measure and compare. As we have seen, Tony did get a lot of things wrong—Cap died, the Hulk came back, and the Skrulls invaded. So even a self-styled futurist can make mistakes. And since his decisions are only as good as his predictions, Tony's inability to know the results of this action casts his decisions in doubt. This doubt, of course, applies to all utilitarian decision making.

Captain America: Duty above All Else

Iron Man and Captain America have long been depicted as seeing the world differently. The Civil War, though, brought this ethical conflict to the forefront of the Marvel Universe. While Tony exemplifies utilitarianism, Cap provides a shining example of *deontology*, which judges the morality of actions in and of themselves according to general principles or duties rather than consequences.[7] In the case of Tony's stopping the Crimson Dynamo's heart, Cap presumably regarded this as a violation of the principle not to kill. As far as Cap is concerned, the "expediency" Tony cited does not work as a justification. The conflict between deontology and utilitarianism is often put in terms of the "right" and the "good," in which the good is a quantity to be maximized while the right is something to be adhered to. Stopping the Dynamo's heart may have been the most expedient way to a good result, but to Cap it simply wasn't the right thing to do.

When deontologists (like Cap) criticize utilitarians (like Tony) for letting "the ends justify the means," they are implying that certain means to an end should never be taken, regardless of how good the consequences would be. No matter how worthy an end—even saving lives—some measures should not be taken as a matter of principle. In the real world, torturing terror suspects and placing wiretaps on phones are prime examples; in the Civil War, we see examples such as building the Negative Zone and enlisting the Thunderbolts. Such actions, considered intrinsically wrong, cannot be justified by their consequences, but rather taint those otherwise noble ends. To be sure, deontologists do not entirely dismiss the importance of consequences, but they do regard principles as important also.

One advantage that deontology seems to have over utilitarianism is that it doesn't require us to calculate and compare the good and bad consequences of every decision. Cap wouldn't have worked out the pros and cons of inviting the Thunderbolts to his cause. Rather, he just never would have considered it, because he would regard it as wrong to deal with confirmed killers. (He ultimately rejects the Punisher's offer to join the anti-registration movement for the same reason.)[8] But this neglects the complexity of distinguishing right from wrong. When Cap says to Tony that "what's right is right," or tells Sharon Carter (regarding the pro-registration forces) that "what they're doing is wrong, plain and simple," his simple language obscures the fact that a tremendous amount of deliberation and judgment goes into determining what is right in any given situation.[9] Instead of calculating positive and negative effects on utility, however, the deontologist weighs various principles and duties against each other (and even against consequences).

Furthermore, deontology avoids the contingent nature of utilitarian ethics, by which a change in circumstances can flip a moral judgment one way or another. Tony was originally opposed to registration, citing the risks to heroes' loved ones, morale, and incentives to continue to serve as heroes.[10] Once he was convinced that the registration act would pass, however, he signed on as its figurehead, telling Peter Parker, "I have to take the lead in making the other powers register. If I don't, someone else worse will. And frankly . . . I think it's the right thing to do at this point."[11] From a utilitarian point of view this is admirable: he adjusted to circumstances and did the best with the cards he was dealt as they changed. To a deontologist, though, right and wrong do not depend on circumstances but on principle. Cap was steadfast in opposing registration, not out of stubbornness, but out of a style of judgment that does not depend on the state of the world at any given time. Even when he surrendered at the end of *Civil War*, it was not because he changed his mind about registration, but because he realized his efforts had strayed from their original purpose: "We're not fighting for the people anymore . . . we're just fighting."[12] When Iron Man visits him in his cell at Ryker's, Cap tells him, "we maintained the principles we swore to defend and protect. You sold your principles."[13] It would be more precise, though, to say that Tony and Cap simply had different overarching principles to begin with, representing the good and the right. Each fought for his principle to the end—and with conviction.

Convicted Heroes

It's easy to point out the differences between utilitarianism and deontology, but we should also point out their similarities. (This will prove especially useful when we get to discussing virtue ethics and Thor.) We've already mentioned one similarity: both utilitarianism and deontology require judgment, albeit of different kinds. Utilitarianism demands the anticipation, evaluation, and comparison of every possible result of every option, while deontology requires the consideration and balancing of every principle and duty involved in a situation. Neither process can be done perfectly—and waiting while a person tries can result in disaster. Choices have to be made, and sometimes a person has to use judgment to make them once the time for deliberation runs out. As Tony said during the battle with the Hulk, "Every day I choose between courses of action that could affect millions, even billions of lives. With stakes that high, how dare I decide? But at this point, doing nothing is a decision in and of itself."[14]

Ethical decision making of either type, utilitarian or deontological, requires conviction to make it effective. Coming to the best decision is one thing, but it's worthless if the person doesn't follow through with it. Despite Iron Man and Captain America's differences, they both share tremendous conviction. Talking to Cap's corpse after his assassination on the courtroom steps, Tony confesses, "I knew that I would be put in the position of taking charge of this side of things. Because if not me, who? Who else was there? No one. So I sucked it up. I did what you do. I committed. . . . It was the right thing to do!"[15]

As usual, Cap gives a more eloquent speech to demonstrate his conviction, this time to Spider-Man as he considers abandoning Tony to side with Cap:

> Doesn't matter what the press says. Doesn't matter what the politicians or the mobs say. Doesn't matter if the whole country decides that something wrong is something right. This nation was founded on one principle above all else: the requirement that we stand up for what we believe, no matter the odds or the consequences. When the mob and the press and the whole world tell you to move, your job is to plant yourself like a tree beside the river of truth, and tell the whole world—"No, *you* move."[16]

Of course, no one would ever doubt Captain America's conviction, but my point is more general: that conviction does not depend on one's moral philosophy. As Cap says, "If you believe it, you stand up for it."[17]

Understanding the importance of judgment and conviction can also help us see through the misconception that deontological ethics (such as Cap's) views the world as "black and white" with no "shades of gray," simply because it trucks in absolute terms like "right or wrong" instead of relative terms like "better or worse." For utilitarians, the only right decision is the "best" one, the one that results in the most net positive results—every other choice is wrong. When Sharon asks Cap, regarding the registration act, "If Captain America doesn't follow the law, then who does?" Cap replies, "The issue isn't black and white, and those are the only colors the law can see," as opposed to the broader deontological concepts of justice and liberty that he values.[18] But once you see past the simple rules—what contemporary philosopher and economist Deirdre McCloskey mocks as doing ethics by "three-by-five-inch card"—and recognize the role of judgment in ethical decision making, then neither utilitarianism nor deontology is black and white.[19] The only thing deserving of that term is conviction, the determination to stand by one's moral choices, which can often be confused with stubbornness. In fact, though, conviction is a virtue.

Verily, a Fine Segue!

Another thing utilitarianism and deontology have in common is their focus on action: determining the right thing in do in any particular situation. But our third school of ethics, *virtue ethics*, focuses on the actor instead, emphasizing enduring character traits that good (or virtuous) people possess, such as honesty, courage, and resolve—all of them hallmarks of a hero.[20] Iron Man and Captain America display these virtues, of course, but their virtues do not account for how they make moral decisions. For an example of virtue ethics, we turn to our third Avenger Prime, Thor.

The Odinson lives by a code of honor, adhering to the highest standards of bravery, loyalty, and honesty, and these ideals motivate his actions. He does not weigh the positive and negative effects of alternatives like Tony does, but rather lets his instincts guide him to the right action. In this way Thor resembles Cap, in that they both do the "right thing." Of course, they do it for different reasons, though: Cap does the right thing because it represents his duties or principles, and Thor because it represents his character.

Because of his well-earned slumber after breaking the seemingly endless cycle of Ragnarok (the death of the gods), Thor missed out on the Civil War. When he returned to Earth, though, he discovered both Captain America's death and Iron Man's part in creating the clone of Thor (as well as his other questionable decisions). When Iron Man meets him to welcome him back to Earth as his friend and then to "urge" him to register, Thor recounts Tony's deeds during the superhero battle, describing them as offenses against virtue:

> You have hunted down those we once fought beside and called comrades. Killed or imprisoned those who opposed you, regardless of their previous loyalties. . . . You took my genetic code and, without my permission, without my knowledge, used it to create an abomination—an aberration—an insult—and this you told the world was me. You defiled my body, desecrated my trust, violated everything that I am. Is this how you define friendship?[21]

Thor does not address the motives or rationale for Tony's actions, but instead his violation of the basic concepts of camaraderie, loyalty, integrity, respect, trust, and friendship. A good person does not act against these virtues, as Thor says to Tony with eloquent language—and devastating force. Instead, good people embody these virtues, which are an essential part of their character, and manifest themselves in their decisions, intentions, and actions (although not necessarily perfectly).[22]

On the first anniversary of Captain America's death, Thor visits his gravesite and summons the spirit of his fallen comrade. After offering to avenge Cap's murder (an offer that is declined), Thor pays tribute, again in the language of virtue, specifically the virtues of honor and friendship:

> I have lived many ages of men, Steven. Centuries without end. I have seen many great men, and known countless honors. But the greatest honor of this ancient and tired soul has been the privilege of fighting beside you, and calling you my friend.[23]

Again, Thor does not care about Cap's dedication to duty or principle, but how well that leads him to live up to virtues that Thor regards as worthy of a hero, a warrior, and a friend.

Of course, it is not merely others whom Thor holds up to the standards of virtue, but first and foremost himself. He is unwavering in his fairness, as when he approached a demonic, rampaging Asgardian with an open hand before engaging and defeating him in battle, and then accepted exile from Asgard once it was revealed that his vanquished foe was none other than Bor, his grandfather and previous king.[24] He is unflinching in his courage, such as when he swears during the Siege of Asgard, after being beaten down by Norman Osborn and his Dark Avengers, "I will not run from you, Osborn, not your minions. I will not hide. I will defend my home and the home of my father . . . with my very last breath."[25] He has a profound sense of honor and justice, refusing to kill Bob Reynolds (the Sentry) at the end of the Siege—even when Reynolds begs him to—until Reynolds forces his hand by attacking the Avengers (after which Thor takes his burnt body, wrapped in his cape, and buries it in the sun).[26] And he is fiercely loyal, going so far as to revive his adopted brother Loki following his death during the destruction of Asgard (for which Loki was ultimately responsible but later repented).[27]

Of course, many heroes exemplify these traits, including Iron Man and Captain America, but Thor acts this way for the sake of these virtues, rather than out of the expectation of good consequences or respect for duty or principle. Thor strives to be a good person, a virtuous person. For instance, at the end of *Avengers Prime*, Thor reclaims the Twilight Sword with which Hela (the goddess of death) had reshaped the nine realms, but he refuses to use it himself. He could have restored Asgard to its former glory, before it was destroyed in the last Ragnarok, then restored over Broxton, Oklahoma, and later destroyed again in the Siege.[28] But he tells Amora (the Enchantress), "To use this unholy power for my own ends would make me the same demon she is."[29] And that "same demon"—someone who uses infinite power for his own ends, or even for what he predicts would be the best for everybody—isn't who Thor strives to be.

Ethicists Assemble!

Can we conclude, therefore, that virtue ethics has nothing in common with utilitarianism and deontology? Absolutely not— all three ethical approaches can be seen as ways to determine the right thing to do or the right way to live, whether approached through action or character. And they often reach the same conclusions when it comes to very general topics such as murder and lying, though they may have different things to say on specific cases. For instance, utilitarianism might be more permissive of some well-meaning lies than deontology or virtue ethics.

Still, no matter which ethical framework you choose to adopt, you need to exercise judgment to apply it to specific circumstances. You also need conviction to stand by your decision in the face of criticism from others or doubts from within. As much as our Avengers Prime may differ in terms of their basic moral philosophy, they share the same capacity for sound judgment and unshakable conviction. Ultimately they serve as examples to those of us who aspire to be heroes in our own lives—but can't afford the tuition at Avengers Academy!

NOTES

1. See, for example, *Avengers Academy* #10 (May 2011), reprinted in *Avengers Academy: When Will We Use This in the Real World?* (2011), and discussed here: http://www.comicsprofessor.com/2011/03/superhuman-ethics-class-is-in-session-in-avengers-academy-10.html.

2. *Avengers Prime* #1–5 (August 2010–March 2011), reprinted in *Avengers Prime* (2011).

3. See . . . well, most all Marvel comics since 2006, but especially *Civil War* (2007), *World War Hulk* (2008), *Secret Invasion* (2009), and *Siege* (2010), plus dozens (if not hundreds) of tie-in comics. (Go ahead, read them, I'll wait.)

4. See Bentham's *An Introduction to the Principles of Morals and Legislation* (1781), available at http://www.utilitarianism.com/jeremy-bentham/index.html.

5. Utilitarianism is a specific form of *consequentialism*, which judges the morality of actions by some aspect of their consequences, such as goodness (as in utilitarianism) or equality (as in egalitarianism). For a thorough discussion, see Walter Sinnott-Armstrong, "Consequentialism," *Stanford Encyclopedia of Philosophy*, http://plato.stanford.edu/entries/consequentialism.

6. *Iron Man*, vol. 4, #7 (June 2006), reprinted in *Iron Man: Execute Program* (2007). At the end of the story line (#12, November 2006), to avoid being forced to kill Cap by mental control, Tony stops his own heart, trusting that he would be revived as he did for the Dynamo.

7. See Larry Alexander and Michael Moore, "Deontological Ethics," *Stanford Encyclopedia of Philosophy*, http://plato.stanford.edu/entries/ethics-deontological.

8. *Civil War* #6 (December 2006). On the other hand, he allowed Wolverine into the Avengers despite telling Tony, "He's a murderer" (*New Avengers*, vol. 1, #6, June 2005, reprinted in *New Avengers: Breakout*, 2006). I would like to think that a soldier like Cap knows the difference between someone who kills in the heat of battle and someone who does the same for personal gain (like the Thunderbolts) or vengeance (like the Punisher); for more on this theme, see the chapter "The Avengers and S.H.I.E.L.D.: The Problem with Proactive Superheroics" by Arno Bogaerts in this volume.

9. *Iron Man/Captain America: Casualties of War* (February 2007), reprinted in *Civil War: Iron Man* (2007); *Captain America*, vol. 5, #22 (November 2006), reprinted in *Civil War: Captain America* (2007).

10. See *Amazing Spider-Man* #529–531 (April–June 2006), reprinted in *Civil War: The Road to Civil War* (2007).

11. *Amazing Spider-Man* #532, reprinted in *Civil War: Amazing Spider-Man* (2007).

12. *Civil War* #7 (January 2007).

13. *Civil War: The Confession* (May 2007), reprinted in *Civil War: Iron Man* (2007).

14. *World War Hulk* #4 (November 2007).

15. *Civil War: The Confession*.

16. *Amazing Spider-Man* #537 (December 2006), reprinted in *Civil War: Amazing Spider-Man*.

17. Captain America to Iron Man, from *Iron Man/Captain America: Casualties of War*.

18. *Captain America*, vol. 5, #22.

19. Deirdre McCloskey, *The Bourgeois Virtues: Ethics for an Age of Commerce* (Chicago: University of Chicago Press, 2006), 263.

20. See Rosalind Hursthouse, "Virtue Ethics," *Stanford Encyclopedia of Philosophy*, http://plato.stanford.edu/entries/ethics-virtue.

21. *Thor*, vol. 3, #3 (November 2007), reprinted in *Thor by J. Michael Straczynski Vol. 1* (2008).

22. For more on virtue and imperfection, see the chapter titled "Cap's Kooky Quartet: Is Rehabilitation Possible?" by Andrew Terjesen in this volume.

23. *Thor*, vol. 3, #11 (November 2008), reprinted in *Thor by J. Michael Straczynski Vol. 2* (2009). For more on the ancient Greek meaning of friendship, see the chapter titled "Gods, Beasts, and Political Animals: Why the Avengers Assemble" by Tony Spanakos in this volume.

24. *Thor*, vol. 3, #600 (April 2009), reprinted in *Thor by J. Michael Straczynski Vol. 2*. (After issue #12, the series was renumbered at #600 to commemorate the anniversary of the title.)

25. *Siege* #2 (April 2010).

26. *Siege* #4 (June 2010).

27. *Thor*, vol. 3, #617 (January 2011), reprinted in *Thor: The World Eaters* (2011).

28. He could have also erased the *Twilight* books and movies from existence. You know, for the irony.

29. *Avengers Prime* #5 (March 2011).

SHINING THE LIGHT ON THE DARK AVENGERS

Sarah Donovan and Nick Richardson

Formed in the aftermath of the Secret Invasion, the team of Avengers assembled by Norman Osborn—and known to comic book readers as the Dark Avengers—appear to work for the public good. Shedding his alter ego, the Green Goblin, Osborn became the head of H.A.M.M.E.R. (the successor to S.H.I.E.L.D.) by promoting his role in the defeat of the Skrull invasion—as well as pointing out that Tony Stark, Nick Fury, S.H.I.E.L.D., and the (old) Avengers had failed to prevent it in the first place. Since the American public believes that they are "real" Avengers, the Dark Avengers can piggyback on their predecessors' squeaky-clean reputation and get away with all sorts of wicked deeds. Made up of villains posing as classic Avengers like Hawkeye and Ms. Marvel, the Dark Avengers do protect the public good after the Atlanteans attack Melrose, but they also engage in behavior unbecoming of true Avengers. For instance, Osborn forms an alliance with the evil Cabal; in retaliation for the attack on Melrose, the Sentry (who was a "real" Avenger as well) kills all of the Atlantean terrorists; and the "new" Hawkeye murders the Sentry's wife on Osborn's orders.[1]

In public, the Dark Avengers appear to be good, but in reality they are not. For philosophers, this raises questions. Is it necessary to *be* good, or is it enough to *appear* to be good? If you could get away with being bad while appearing to be good, would you do it? And what do we think of people who do get away with it?

Plato and the Ancient Greek Avengers

In the *Republic*, Plato (429–347 BCE) creates a character out of his teacher Socrates (469–399 BCE), who argues that when people are just, it is because they are guided by something divine and perfect.[2] Steve Rogers, also known as Captain America, embodies this belief; his actions seem to be guided and motivated by a profound sense of justice. He has exceptional strength, endurance, and discipline, which he could use to take what he wants by force, yet he chooses to be a soldier, a superhero, and an Avenger, serving the public good instead of his own. Cap's deep patriotism is an example of his dedication to norms that he regards as greater than himself.

Another of Plato's characters in the *Republic*, Thrasymachus, argues instead that we are only good when we think we will benefit from it. Nothing greater than us determines our actions except our own advantage, especially avoiding getting caught doing the wrong thing. Norman Osborn exemplifies this view when he becomes the head of H.A.M.M.E.R. and puts together his team of Avengers to serve his own nefarious purposes. Though the Dark Avengers do some good, it is merely a cover for Osborn's greater plans. Osborn does not believe in any sense of "justice" beyond his own advantage.

But what does it mean to believe in concepts of goodness or justice that are above or beyond us? To answer this, we move into the realm of *metaphysics*, the study of that which is beyond the physical, things that can't be touched, such as gods or the soul. Plato's theory of the Forms is a classic example of a metaphysical theory. Plato believed that the Forms are immaterial, perfect entities that are the blueprints for all things that exist on earth. Physical objects, by contrast, are copies (with differing degrees of imperfections) of the Forms.

According to Plato's metaphysics, reality is not what we think. The world of the Forms is the true reality, whereas our world is an inferior realm of change. In his famous *allegory of the cave*, Plato likens our knowledge of the world around us to that of prisoners in a cave, staring at shadows on the wall.[3] The prisoners mistakenly think the shadows are the highest reality, unaware of that which makes the shadows themselves. Likewise, if we are ignorant of the Forms, we will mistakenly think the material world is the highest reality.

Plato urges us to "leave the cave" and gain knowledge of the Forms. After all, we can only be good and just by understanding the Form of the Good and the Form of the Just. Once again, Steve Rogers exemplifies what it means to believe in universal, eternal values such as the Forms. At the end of the Civil War, Rogers, the leader of the anti-registration movement, stands down and is taken into custody. When Tony Stark visits him at the Raft, the maximum-security installation at Ryker's Island, Rogers lambasts Stark for beginning a bloody war that was born out of Stark's ego, rather than any higher ideals, like freedom. We see that Rogers is guided by principles outside of himself when he says to Stark, "Who made you the moral compass of us?"[4] Rogers implies here that there is a general code of ethics that stands apart from humans (and therefore is not created by us) but to which we must conform. This same kind of thinking underlies any belief in ideals and principles. Again we see this when Rogers says to Stark, "We maintained the principles we swore to defend and protect. You sold your principles. You lost this before it started."[5] In short, Rogers can say that he has taken the moral high ground because there really *is* a metaphysical "high ground" to take.

Does Might Make Right?

While Captain America would presumably agree with some metaphysical theory about goodness and justice (though not necessarily Plato's), Norman Osborn clearly would not. For example, when he gives an elaborate TV interview to defend his public image, Osborn acts only for his own good and for the purpose of appearing good to the American people.[6] Osborn is a modern-day Thrasymachus. In the *Republic*, after Socrates argues that justice can only be understood by reference to a metaphysical Form, Thrasymachus counters by saying that "justice is nothing other than the advantage of the stronger."[7] For Thrasymachus (and Osborn), there are no metaphysical Forms against which to measure or judge our actions. Instead, justice is simply about winning at all costs.

Let's set Norman Osborn aside for the moment in order to focus on the members of his Avengers team, who appear to be actual, well-known Avengers. In fact, though, the general public would be horrified to learn their true identities and criminal backgrounds. For instance, the identity of Ms. Marvel is taken by Moonstone (Karla Sofen), who, among other evil deeds, killed her own mother, joined the Masters of Evil, and fought against the Avengers. Daken, Wolverine's twisted son, assumes his father's identity though he's been killing people since he was a child (more indiscriminately than his father has). Hawkeye is really Bullseye, one of Daredevil's prominent and most psychotic enemies, and Spider-Man is Venom (remember Spidey's black costume?).

All of these "heroes" pose as other people who are widely regarded as good, and thus they are seen by the public as the defenders of goodness and justice. We know, of course, that these Dark Avengers are *unjust* in a strong sense of the word— the question is, should we care? Is Thrasymachus right that justice is merely the advantage of the stronger?

Are the Dark Avengers
Evil or Simply Bold?

Another of Plato's characters in the *Republic*, Glaucon, illustrates Thrasymachus's view with a story about the ring of Gyges.[8] In this story, a shepherd comes across a chasm in the middle of a field in which he finds a hollow bronze horse that entombs a dead man wearing a gold ring. The shepherd takes the ring and discovers that it makes him invisible (think Tolkien, but before the common era). He uses the power of the ring to kill the king and take over the kingdom. Through the ring he has gained a superpower, which he could use for just or wicked actions— exactly like the Dark Avengers can (as well as the real ones).

What would happen if there were two such rings, and you gave one to a just person and the other to an unjust person? Glaucon suggests that "no one, it seems, would be so incorruptible that he would stay on the path of justice or stay away from other people's property."[9] In other words, both the just and the unjust person would do bad things; it would simply take the just person a bit longer.

Glaucon goes further, saying that most people would look down upon the person unwilling to commit injustice. If a person was given the opportunity to be invisible, and did not take the opportunity, then that person would "be thought wretched and stupid by everyone aware of the situation, though, of course, they'd praise him in public, deceiving each other for fear of suffering injustice."[10] Glaucon suggests that while we would never admit it publicly, we think that people are fools if they are good when no one else is watching. So in fact he would claim that on some level we admire people like the Dark Avengers.

Glaucon concludes that most people believe the life of an unjust and wicked person is actually better (in nonmoral terms) than that of a just person. So not only do we admire the Dark Avengers, but we believe our life would be better if we were one of them. To demonstrate this, Glaucon sets up a thought experiment with two scenarios. First, imagine a perfectly unjust person who is granted a reputation for being just and, no matter what he does, is able to explain his actions from within his narrative of being a just person. Second, imagine a perfectly just person who never does anything unjust, but who is given a reputation for profound injustice. He will always act justly, but will always be thought to be unjust.

Glaucon's experiment pushes us to ask ourselves whether "being" just is important enough to us that we would accept the second scenario. In other words, if you only had the two options of being just and appearing unjust, or being unjust and appearing just, which would you choose? Do you care enough about being just that you would accept being shunned by your family, friends, and society (in which case you accept Socrates's view)? Or do you care more about power and the praise you get from those around you (in which case you accept Thrasymachus's view)?

The Dark Avengers all have "magic rings," so to speak. They all appear to be good because they are dressed up like Avengers, but they do bad things that the general public does not know about. The short run of *Dark Avengers* abounds with examples of hidden violent actions that the average person would consider morally despicable. For instance, Norman Osborn gives Bullseye, posing as Hawkeye, the order to murder the Sentry's wife, Lindy. Bullseye is more than happy to throw Lindy out of a helicopter and then claim that she committed suicide.[11] We can see what the Dark Avengers, and especially Osborn, do when they have the power of invisibility, hiding behind the identities of legitimate Avengers, but the truly scary thought is how readily they were accepted as such.

No One Needs to Know

Like Glaucon's example of the unjust person who is granted a reputation for justice, Osborn consistently works to maintain a positive public image for himself and his team. For example, some members of the newly assembled Dark Avengers suggest that they make the public safe by going after Tony Stark, to which Osborn replies, "No. For now, Tony Stark is a court of law matter. Kicking a man while he's down is hardly a way to win over the public." Bullseye asks, "Who cares about that on any level?" Osborn responds, "I do. So you do, too."[12] After the Dark Avengers' first public appearance, Osborn tells them, "Let me make something perfectly clear. . . . None of you—I mean none of you—talk to the media ever again."[13] Osborn plans to control every aspect of the Dark Avengers' public image, because the "rings" must be polished if they are to work properly.

Osborn's concern with the public image of the Dark Avengers continues when Clint Barton (the genuine Hawkeye) claims on television that "Norman Osborn is employing criminals to do his black ops dirty work, right here in the United States."[14] Barton says that Osborn himself is "a criminal sociopath. Most people don't even know, or seem to have forgotten, but he used to be the murderer known as the Green Goblin."[15] Of course, Osborn goes on television to dispel Barton's claims. While not denying that he was the Green Goblin (but pointing out Barton's criminal past), Osborn appeals to public pity and says that he was once mentally ill but is now healed. He claims that he sought therapy and even took medication to relieve his "condition." To bolster his appeal he says, "And really, do you think for a second that the president of the United States and the Joint Chiefs of Staff would allow a murderous costumed maniac to lead an important initiative in this, the most important time in our history?"[16] Osborn knows that he must manipulate public perception so that he and the Dark Avengers can pursue their own unjust agenda.

While Osborn works hard to maintain a squeaky-clean image for the Dark Avengers, Barton is not the only one who knows the true identity of some of the Dark Avengers. Fellow villain Morgan Le Fay knows, as does Maria Hill, former deputy director of S.H.I.E.L.D. After being fired by Osborn,

Hill tells him that she needs to talk to him in person: "I wanted to look you right in the eye. I wanted this moment with you. I wanted to tell you that when you do crash and burn—and . . . oh you will—I will be there when it happens. Laughing my ass off." At the end of the first issue of *Dark Avengers*, Hill stands with Nick Fury and others who understand the true nature of the Dark Avengers. As Fury says to his newly assembled team, "You will be my army. The world needs us. These are dark and desperate times."[17]

Recall that Glaucon (channeling Thrasymachus) asserts that most people would love the opportunity to do what they want and take what they want for themselves but also maintain a reputation for being good and just. So according to Glaucon, we are actually jealous of the Dark Avengers and their blatant lack of morals. If you disagree with Glaucon, then you probably believe that there is a deeper sense in which we are "good" or "bad." While you might not wish to appear unjust in order to be just, you would do it. And, of course, so do some of the characters in *Dark Avengers*.

Being Just

The real Avengers' Ms. Marvel (Carol Danvers), the Dark Avengers' Captain Marvel (Noh-Varr), and dual Avenger (and Greek god) Ares are willing to risk everything—reputation and life—in order to be just. When Osborn tells Danvers that he is the new head of the Avengers, she refuses to work with him, saying, "No one worth a damn will side with you, Norman. There will be no Avengers. None."[18] So strong are her convictions that she goes AWOL from her military position to avoid working with Osborn. She would rather be perceived as having abandoned her duties than merely appear to be a just and good soldier by working with Osborn. But Danvers is a "true" Avenger, so we wouldn't expect anything less.

Likewise, Noh-Varr leaves the Dark Avengers as soon as he finds out that his fellow Dark Avengers are actually criminals. He discovers this when Moonstone, posing as Ms. Marvel, hurries to turn on the TV to hear Osborn's interview shortly after seducing Noh-Varr. She says to him, "I'm dying to see how Norman sells the fact that he put together a team of psychotic criminals and murderers and calls them Avengers."[19] Noh-Varr is genuinely shocked as he says, "He put together what?"[20] That night Noh-Varr defects from the Dark Avengers and goes into hiding. Everyone who shuns the Dark Avengers seems to think that there is something deeper to being good than simply being on the winning side.

Ares is yet another example of someone who would rather be just than merely appear to be just. When he joined the Dark Avengers, he, like Noh-Varr, was naïve in his belief that he and Osborn served together on the side of justice. After the real Ms. Marvel refuses to join the Dark Avengers, and discovers that Ares did, she says to Ares while pointing at Osborn, "Do you know who he is?" Ares responds, "He's the warrior who bested my own enemy in battle." Along with the general public, Ares thinks that Osborn is a hero who stopped the Skrull invasion. During the Siege of Asgard, however, Ares discovers that Osborn had lied to him and used him. He attacks Osborn, saying, "And I told you what I would do, Osborn! I told you true! I'm going to pull off your head, armor and all."[21] The Sentry steps in to defend Osborn, literally tearing Ares in half. Ares gives more than his reputation to be just—he gives his life. (But he's a god—he gets better.)

Just How Dark Are the Dark Avengers?

When you do the "right thing," is it because you think you are being watched, or is it because you have a deeper belief about "right" and "wrong" that guides your actions? If, like Osborn, you were given the opportunity to direct a team of corrupt super-heroes, would you avoid the temptation to punish your nemesis, accumulate wealth, and settle a few scores? If no one knew, and you were guaranteed that no one would know, what would you do? If you commissioned these acts, would you feel guilty? If you would feel guilty, then you are either a truly virtuous person or a great fool. Unfortunately, philosophy has no scientific method for determining which you are, and so we are left wondering: what do we *really* think about the Dark Avengers?

NOTES

1. All of this occurred in the *Dark Avengers* series, which lasted sixteen issues from March 2009 to July 2010, and has been collected in the hardcover *Dark Avengers* (2011) as well as separate trade paperbacks.

2. In Plato, *Complete Works*, ed. John M. Cooper (Indianapolis: Hackett, 1997). Standard pagination is given whenever Plato is quoted, so you can find the relevant passages in any reputable translation.

3. See Book VII of the *Republic*.

4. *Civil War: The Confession* (May 2007).

5. Ibid.

6. *Dark Avengers* #5 (August 2009).

7. *Republic*, 338c.

8. Although it is worth noting that Glaucon says that he is supporting Thrasymachus's argument only because he wants Socrates to really defeat it. Glaucon wants to agree with Socrates, but he also wants a good argument. (He may have been the first devil's advocate!) See *Republic*, 357a–b.

9. *Republic*, 360b.

10. Ibid., 360d.

11. *Dark Avengers* #14–15 (April–May 2010). See *Dark Reign: Hawkeye* (2010) for more examples of Bullseye's heinous conduct while wearing Clint Barton's costume.

12. *Dark Avengers* #1 (March 2009).

13. *Dark Avengers* #2 (April 2009).

14. *Dark Avengers* #4 (June 2009).

15. Ibid.

16. *Dark Avengers* #5 (August 2009).

17. *Dark Avengers* #1.

18. Ibid.

19. *Dark Avengers* #5.

20. Ibid.

21. *Siege* #1–2 (March–April 2010), reprinted in *Siege* (2010).

THE AVENGERS:
EARTH'S MIGHTIEST
FAMILY

Jason Southworth and Ruth Tallman

What makes a hero or a villain? Often, when we talk about heroes we focus on their strong character, on the virtues of courage, determination, and self-reliance that make them remarkable. We tend to give them a lot of personal credit for the way they excel in the world. But did you ever stop to think about the people who had a hand in shaping those heroes into the individuals they eventually became?

There is a long tradition in the Marvel Universe of family legacies of heroism and villainy. T'Chaka and his children, T'Challa and Shuri, all served Wakanda as its protector, the Black Panther. Twins Brian and Elizabeth Braddock have made names for themselves as heroes Captain Britain and Psylocke, respectively. Some families have been involved in superheroics and evildoing for generations. The second Captain America's

(Isaiah Bradley's) grandson, Eli Bradley, is carrying on the family legacy as Patriot. On the evil side of the coin, father and son Heinrich and Helmut Zemo have both fought Captain America as Baron Zemo, carrying on a tradition of evil that stretches back twelve generations.

All of these examples are indications that upbringing counts for a lot when it comes to a person's character. Nature—even in the form of radioactive spiders and gamma rays—accounts for the potential of a person to become a hero or a villain, but nurture plays a pivotal role in influencing which path a person will follow. In this chapter, we'll consider the issue of parental responsibility for the actions and characters of children, using examples drawn from decades of Avengers comics.

Of Father and Ultron

We don't have to go very far into the history of the Avengers to see that there are inconsistencies in the manner in which parents are credited or blamed for the way their children turn out. More comic book pages have been spent on the relationship between Hank Pym and Ultron, the living automaton, than on any other parent and child. Pym, the Avenger who holds the record for the most number of aliases (Ant-Man, Giant-Man, Goliath, Yellowjacket, Wasp, and Scientist Supreme), developed a super computer with a human-level intelligence based on Pym's own "brain patterns."[1] Following his creation, Ultron quickly developed self-consciousness and, with it, thoughts of his own. Unfortunately, these thoughts included killing Pym, the rest of the Avengers, and pretty much everyone else.

Some might find it strange to discuss the Hank Pym/Ultron relationship as a parental one, but this is the way people in the Marvel Universe view it. Ultron and Pym explicitly address each other as "father" and "son." Furthermore, when Ultron Mark 12 (the "good" incarnation of Ultron) dies, Pym mourns the death of his "son" and is so distraught that he contemplates suicide (actually holding a gun to his head).[2] Their relationship is like that of many parents and children—for instance, Hank was there for Ultron's creation, and the two reconnected for better and worse after Ultron became his own person. However, Pym never had a chance to influence Ultron's thoughts, and in fact he didn't even know that his "son" had developed self-consciousness until Ultron attacked him for the first time.

So is Hank Pym morally responsible for Ultron's behavior? For the Avengers, the answer is a resounding yes. There are dozens of instances where people have expressed judgment and condemnation of Pym, and he has been explicitly blamed for the death and destruction caused by Ultron. The line of thought seems to be that Hank is responsible because had he not created Ultron, Ultron couldn't have committed his terrible deeds. Ms. Marvel (Carol Danvers) sums up this sentiment best when she thinks, "And you created Ultron so $%#@ you. . . . If you can't [stop him], kill yourself."[3] So there is a strong intuition among the Avengers, and shared by most readers, that Pym did something wrong just by fathering Ultron, even if he had no role in crafting Ultron's "character."

Sometimes the Apples Do Fall Far from the Tree

A tension arises, however, when we consider the case of two other Avengers, Wanda and Pietro Maximoff, known as the Scarlet Witch and Quicksilver. These Avengers didn't come to know their father until they were adults. Their mother, Magda Eisenhardt, left their father while she was pregnant out of fear that harm would come to her children because her husband, Max, had revealed himself to be a mutant. Magda died soon after giving birth, and the twins were placed in the care of a gypsy couple named Django and Marya Maximoff.[4] This is why their surname differs from that of their father, Max Eisenhardt, who later adopted the name Erik Lehnsherr, better known as Magneto.

Magneto's actions as a supervillain and mutant terrorist clearly earn him a place high on the list of the greatest villains of the Marvel Universe. But his fatherhood is much like that of Hank Pym: Magneto contributed his DNA to his children, while Hank donated his brain patterns. After that initial involvement, neither participated in the moral education or character-building of their progeny. Pym was ignorant of Ultron's mental development, and Magneto had no idea where his children were. Yet while Hank is blamed for Ultron, no one has ever given Magneto any credit for fathering two Avengers. The only difference is that Pym is a hero who fathered a villain, and Magneto is a villain who fathered heroes. It is unclear how that fact could affect moral praiseworthiness or blameworthiness, however. The cases seem to be the same in all relevant regards, so we can't have it both ways. If Magneto gets no credit, then Pym should get no blame—and if Pym is held responsible, so should Magneto. So what are we to do? It looks like we are going to need to find something other than mere creation to hang our praise and blame on.

Let's think about the underlying factors that prompt our gut response of wanting to blame Pym. It seems like we react so negatively to Pym's role in creating Ultron because Ultron is so evil, and having a hero for a father just intensifies our visceral response. We think that heroes should have heroic kids, and the jarring juxtaposition of Hank's heroism and Ultron's evil is deeply unsettling. We react to our discomfort by searching for someone to blame, and Hank is the most readily available target. When a villain's child manages to turn out okay, on the other hand, we tend to think simply that the kid got lucky, or had an exceptionally strong character that stopped him from falling victim to the corrupting influence of his evil parent. We don't seem to mind the lack of symmetry when the child is better than the parent; we don't need to blame anyone for anything, and we don't want to give credit to a villainous parent.

Journey to the Center of the Ant

This gives us a psychological explanation for why we want to blame Hank but not praise Magneto, but is this justified or fair? Let's take a look at a paradigmatic example of a hero and his heroic kid to see what we can learn regarding the appropriate designation of parental praise and blame.

Scott Lang (the second Ant-Man, after Pym) is often given considerable credit for his daughter Cassie's success as a superhero (Stature). Earlier in her teens she was a founding member of the Young Avengers, and she went on to become the youngest person knowingly admitted into the Avengers proper in Pym's Mighty Avengers lineup.[5] Praising her father doesn't seem misguided in this case, and a closer look at their relationship should tell us why.

It isn't discussed much anymore, but Scott Lang was first introduced to the Marvel Universe as a criminal. After failing as an electrician, he tried his hand at burglary, failed at that as well, and ended up in jail. He first became Ant-Man using equipment he had stolen from Hank Pym's laboratory in order to rescue the only doctor who could cure Cassie (then a young child) of a heart condition.[6] From that point forward, Lang did everything in his power to teach Cassie the difference between right and wrong, a lesson he stressed he had to learn the hard way. This effort paid off, as Scott succeeded in instilling his daughter with strong moral values, a sense of social responsibility, and a willingness to sacrifice much of her own adolescence to help strangers. Cassie consistently makes it clear that she is a superhero because of the lessons she learned from her father, which is what motivated her to adopt a version of her dad's old costume, both to honor his memory and to make a strong declaration that she is who she is because of Scott Lang. In short, had Cassie not had Scott as a father, it is unlikely that she would have become a superhero.

One way to understand the influence Scott had on Cassie comes to us through the tradition of the Greek philosopher

Aristotle (384–322 BCE). Aristotle believed that while we might have innate tendencies to behave in particular ways, much of our moral character is developed through a process of habitual imitation. Aristotle thought that we learn to be good people by watching and imitating those who have already developed virtuous habits. This idea has been met with renewed philosophical interest in recent years under the name *moral exemplarism.*[7] Moral exemplarists argue that when we spend time with strong moral role models, it is highly likely that we will begin to adopt patterns of behavior that imitate those exemplars. This is exactly what happened in Cassie's case. With Ant-Man as her father and moral exemplar, it is hardly surprising that Cassie became the hero Stature.

The philosophical concept of moral exemplarism helps us figure out what to make of those puzzling tensions regarding parental praise and blame. If we consider the cases of Pym and Ultron, and Magneto and his twin children, through the lens of the Langs, a clearer picture emerges of what determines whether parental praise or blame is actually warranted. Magneto's genes produced great kids, but who cares? Pym's brain waves resulted in an evil robot, but that's not Pym's fault. We shouldn't praise Magneto or blame Pym, because neither of them served as moral (or immoral) exemplars for their children. When we praise Scott Lang, it's not for contributing his genes to Cassie but for giving his daughter a solid moral grounding and setting an example of the way a hero should live and die. Even if Scott weren't Cassie's biological father, he would deserve credit for *raising* Cassie.

So we've finally got an answer: parents deserve praise for the willful effort they put into helping their children become good people, and they deserve blame when they fail to contribute in that way to their children's upbringing—or when they act to influence their kids for the worse, like the elder Baron Zemo did. Parents who are present and active in their children's lives can have a huge impact on the adults they become, as can be seen in many examples throughout Avengers lore.

The Ties That Bind

Through flashbacks, we learn that similar types of childhood experiences shaped Scott Lang's teammate T'Challa, the Black Panther. While he was growing up, T'Challa's father, T'Chaka, was the Black Panther, the leader of their homeland of Wakanda. Although a busy national figure, T'Chaka played a very hands-on role in his son's upbringing. T'Chaka thought it important that from as young an age as possible, his son understand right from wrong and what it means to have people depend on you. To facilitate this, they discussed these matters often, and T'Challa frequently accompanied his father as he conducted business throughout Wakanda. It was on one of these trips that T'Chaka was murdered by Ulysses Klaw. Witnessing his father's death, T'Challa reacted with the instincts his father had worked to develop in him, and was able to turn Klaw's weapon against him, saving countless lives.[8] This is not to give all the credit to T'Chaka, though. T'Challa was also raised by his stepmother, Ramonda, after his biological mother died during childbirth. Ramonda dedicated her life to raising T'Challa as his father wanted, and prevented him from being consumed with rage over T'Chaka's death. To this day, Ramonda is still one of T'Challa's closest advisers, and one of the few people from whom he keeps no secrets.

On the villainous side of things, we have the Barons Zemo. The elder, Heinrich, was a Nazi scientist who fought Captain America during World War II. Although he is best known for being the man responsible for Cap's suspended animation and his sidekick Bucky's apparent death, he also created countless superweapons used to facilitate the Nazi war effort. Zemo was so despised for his cruelty, even by other Germans during the war, that he took to wearing a mask to hide his face (a point that is pretty amusing since he didn't hide his name, so he couldn't have had much anonymity). Heinrich had a son, Helmut, and as you might expect from a Nazi of the first order, Heinrich raised his son to believe that Aryans were the only people of worth. Adding insult to injury, Heinrich was also abusive to Helmut, directing his anger and frustration at being stuck in his mask toward his son.

As you might expect, Helmut didn't grow up to be a stable individual. When he learned that Captain America was still alive, the younger Zemo sought to establish justice—in the perverted form of the concept taught to him by his father—and worked to kill Captain America, first as the Phoenix and later, modifying his father's costume, as a new Baron Zemo, becoming one of the Avengers' greatest foes as well as continuing to plague Rogers and later Bucky (Rogers's successor as Captain America).[9]

The Torch Is Passed

That attention and guidance go a long way to shaping an individual is a lesson the leaders of the Avengers learned early. Iron Man and Captain America have gone out of their way to recruit criminals and troubled individuals into the Avengers family in an attempt to offer them guidance to help them become heroes (and to prevent them from becoming super pains in the ass).

The first major roster change to the team added the Scarlet Witch, Quicksilver, and Hawkeye (Clint Barton), who with Captain America formed "Cap's Kooky Quartet."[10] For those counting at home, that's two terrorists and a thief. A true Avengers fan doesn't need to be told how this turned out: all three reformed and have served in several incarnations of the team. Subsequent criminal additions to the team have included the aforementioned Scott Lang, thief and Russian spy Natasha Romanova (the Black Widow), Ultron's son the Vision (who joined the team in the same issue in which he first appeared as a villain attacking the Wasp), the Swordsman (the first villain defeated by Cap's Kooky Quartet), and Eric O'Grady, the third Ant-Man, who masqueraded as a superhero for personal gain.[11]

Why would Cap, Tony, and the other Avengers risk inviting questionable characters and downright criminals into the group, trusting them to keep their secrets and to cover their backs in dangerous situations? When we think of the mission of the Avengers, our thoughts typically go to the innocent civilians they protect. But it seems another mission of the Avengers has always been to serve as moral exemplars for youngsters in need of direction.[12] Tony Stark had this in mind when he offered Scott Lang his first job out of prison, installing the security system in Avengers Mansion,[13] and the success of Scott and others offers a fair amount of evidence that moral exemplarism actually does work.

Of these examples, Hawkeye is probably the greatest success. He began his career as an Avenger resentful for the oversight, and he is famous for fighting constantly with Captain America. For much of his early career as an Avenger, he thought he did not get enough respect, and he quit the team several times to prove he didn't need help to be a hero. In spite of this distasteful behavior, Captain America kept encouraging him. Over time, Hawkeye became one of the most trusted Avengers, and when it was time to start a second team on the West Coast, the Vision chose Hawkeye to assemble and lead the team.[14] Hawkeye took the lesson of second chances seriously: when the Thunderbolts, a group of supervillains claiming to be reformed, emerged, he supported them, adopting for them the role Captain America had played for him.[15]

At this point, it ought to be clear that a moral exemplar needn't be a parent, or even a blood relative. Our tendency to praise and blame parents for the actions and characters of their children comes from the fact that most parents do serve as moral exemplars for their kids. Parents are usually the people children spend the most time with during their formative years, and it is natural to develop feelings of admiration for those who care for us when we are vulnerable. However, we also know, and this is increasingly clear in our modern world of blended families, that the nurturing, caregiving role is sometimes provided quite well by a nonparent. T'Challa's stepmother, Ramonda, is a great example of this. While not his biological mother, she filled the maternal role in his life and certainly acted as a moral exemplar, alongside as well as after the death of his biological parent. Magneto is Wanda and Pietro's father, but he has never been their moral exemplar—that role was played by Cap and the other Avengers. What is important isn't blood but action. The Avengers have taught us that providing structure, guidance, and a clear model to follow can have wonderful results, and can form lasting, family-strength relationships among the most unlikely of individuals.

Sins of the Father?

In cases like Pym and Magneto, we might be tempted to say that while we can't hold them morally accountable for the way their children turned out, since they weren't involved in their upbringing, maybe we *should* hold them accountable for not being present in their children's lives. To be fair, Pym and Magneto probably need to be let off the hook for this, since Magneto didn't know where his children were or how to find them and Ultron's childhood occurred while Hank was, uh, sleeping. But generally, don't parents have an obligation to raise their kids?

Actually, no, or at least not always. Moral exemplars have an enormous influence on the way their emulators turn out. Raising kids is a tough job, and frankly, not everyone is up to the task. Think about the Baron Zemo legacy. Heinrich's bad example went a long way to shaping Helmut into the deeply troubled, desperately unhappy menace he became. Wouldn't Heinrich have deserved some praise, rather than blame, if he'd recognized that he was just not father material and given his baby to a stable family to raise? Shouldn't we all send Magneto a thank-you card for *not* raising Wanda and Pietro? Think about what the world would be like if they'd grown up hearing bedtime stories of world domination from dear old Dad.

This is a point that some in the Marvel Universe have acknowledged. The villain Count Luchino Nefaria wanted his infant daughter, Giulietta, to have a chance at a normal life that he knew he'd be unable to provide for her. So he gave her to a wealthy couple, Byron and Loretta Frost, to raise as their own. It was only after the Frosts' death, when Nefaria was unable to leave well enough alone and introduced himself to Giulietta as her real father, that she began the downward spiral that eventuated in her becoming the criminal Madame Masque.[16]

Even if you aren't a depraved villain, sometimes the responsible thing to do is to turn your children's upbringing over to someone who is more qualified to give them the help they need. If you think about it, most parents do this to a limited extent. We send our kids to school to gain knowledge we are ill equipped to give them. We help them acquire skills we ourselves lack by paying piano teachers and soccer coaches to fill in where we fall short. And when a child needs extra help, we'll employ a psychologist or a speech therapist, or even send the child to a special school to get what he or she needs. No one blames the parents of deaf children for sending them away to a specialized school for the hearing impaired. If anything, it is often seen as a noble sacrifice, especially if the children are separated from their loving parents more than they would be at a standard school.

There are clear parallels to these ideas in the Marvel Universe. Professor Xavier and the other leaders of the X-Men are in the business of raising other people's children for them, but we don't blame those kids' parents for sending them to the Xavier School for the Gifted. On the contrary, we are pleased that these children's parents recognized their own inability to offer their mutant children the guidance they need as they learn to cope with and control their powers, and we are happy that they are willing to sacrifice a close parental relationship with their kids in order to give them the best opportunities available.

In the real world, parents who give their children to the state or to a relative to raise are often judged harshly for failing as parents. While there are surely less virtuous reasons for giving up one's parental responsibilities—selfishness or laziness, to name a couple—in some cases, placing one's biological child into hands you know are more capable than your own can be the best and bravest thing a parent can do. This trope is as old as Moses and the bulrushes, and it is something that certainly bears remembering today, when we consider the various forms parental praise and blame can take.

Let There Be an Ending!

The Avengers are one of the elite superhero teams in the Marvel Universe, and the best, brightest, and most powerful heroes would be honored to join the team. Yet Captain America and Iron Man have always made it their business to recruit "wild cards," young, directionless individuals, often with sketchy pasts. They take a chance on these young people, and through the powerful guidance and support the team can provide, morally questionable individuals are transformed into the Earth's mightiest protectors. Especially given that many of these individuals had less than heroic biological parents—can it get any worse than Magneto?—we now have clear evidence that the people who mentored you, rather than those who sired you, have a more profound effect on the way you turn out. And because of this, praise and blame should not be given automatically to one's biological parents, but to one's intellectual or moral "parents," whether those are the same individuals or not. Keep this in mind when thinking about Tigra's young son William: which is worse for him, having a Skrull posing as Hank Pym as the biological father (complete with Pym's DNA), or the real Pym as a nurturing father?[17] (Uh, maybe Magneto's available?)

NOTES

1. As seen in a flashback in *Avengers*, vol. 1, #58 (November 1968), reprinted in *Essential Avengers Vol. 3* (2001).

2. *West Coast Avengers*, vol. 2, #14 (November 1986), reprinted in *Avengers: West Coast Avengers—Sins of the Past* (2011).

3. *Mighty Avengers*, vol. 1, #4 (August 2007), reprinted in *Mighty Avengers Vol. 1: The Ultron Initiative* (2007).

4. *Vision and the Scarlet Witch*, vol. 2, #12 (September 1986), reprinted in *Avengers: Vision and the Scarlet Witch—A Year in the Life* (2010).

5. Rage was technically younger, as he was fourteen, but when his true age was discovered he was demoted to the New Warriors.

6. *Marvel Premiere* #47–48 (April–May 1979).

7. For a modern take on moral exemplarism, see Linda Zagzebski, "Exemplarist Virtue Theory," *Metaphilosophy* 41 (2010): 49–52.

8. This story has been told many times, most recently in *Black Panther*, vol. 4, #1–6 (April–September 2005), reprinted in *Black Panther: Who Is the Black Panther* (2009).

9. He was Phoenix in *Captain America*, vol. 1, #168 (reprinted in *Essential Captain America Vol. 4*, 2008), and the new Baron Zemo in *Captain America*, vol. 1, #275.

10. *Avengers*, vol. 1, #16 (May 1965), reprinted in *Essential Avengers Vol. 1* (1998). Iron Man attempted to recruit Namor in the same issue, but he refused to join. While Namor might not be a villain (Marvel characters and readers are split on this one), everyone agrees he has a serious anger problem that he could use some help getting under control.

11. *Avengers*, vol. 1, #19 (August 1965), #36 (January 1967), #57 (October 1968), #100 (June 1972), and #195 (May 1980), respectively. (All but #195 are reprinted in the *Essential Avengers* volumes.)

12. On redemption, see the chapters titled "Forgivers Assemble!" by Daniel P. Malloy and "Cap's Kooky Quartet: Is Rehabilitation Possible?" by Andrew Terjesen in this volume.

13. *Avengers*, vol. 1, #181 (March 1979), reprinted in *Avengers: Nights of Wundagore* (2009).

14. *Avengers*, vol. 1, #243 (May 1984).

15. See *Thunderbolts* #22 and *Avengers*, vol. 3, #12 (both January 1999, the latter reprinted in *Avengers Assemble Vol. 2*, 2005).

16. *Iron Man*, vol. 1, #18 (October 1969), reprinted in *Essential Iron Man Vol. 3* (2008).

17. See, for instance, *Avengers Academy* #7 (December 2010), reprinted in *Avengers Academy: When Will We Use This in the Real World?* (2011).

PART TWO

WHO IS AN AVENGER?

SUPERHERO IDENTITY: CASE STUDIES IN THE AVENGERS

Stephen M. Nelson

You're in a comic book store and you see a display of *Avengers* comics from the past five decades. Does it seem a little strange that the founding members on the early covers are still around, half a century later, looking pretty much the same? Do you wonder: *are* they the same superheroes? Of course they are, you say—take Iron Man, for instance. He may have different armor on the covers of the first issues of volumes 1 and 4 of *Avengers* (September 1963 and July 2010, respectively), but they're both Tony Stark underneath, so what's the problem?

What may seem obvious at first, though, gets puzzling when we look at some of the other Avengers and the changes they've gone through over the years. Two different kinds of cases in particular challenge our initial clear-cut answer. First, we have superheroes who have been "played" by different people, such as Captain America. Second, there are people who have been many different superheroes, such as Henry "Hank" Pym. Both kinds of cases pose problems about *identity*, or what it is to be a particular superhero. Can one person be many superheroes, and can one superhero be many people? Luckily, we have some philosophical tools that we can bring to bear on these issues, stemming from investigations into the nature of *personal identity*, or what it is to be a person.

It's All about Bodies, Right?

Concerns about the notion of identity, personal or otherwise, come up in the field of *metaphysics*, where philosophers puzzle about the nature of reality. The word "identity" has different uses, but the one that's important in metaphysics is the kind that is also of interest in mathematics. We even call it *numerical identity*, since it is what we use to talk about two things really being one and the same thing across a span of time. For example, you might discover that the woman who just waved to you and the woman who sold you your first car are actually one and the same woman. Another way we could say this is that those women are *identical*.

When philosophers discuss the issue of personal identity, or what it is to be one and the same person over a span of time, we do so by proposing theories that attempt to get at the essence of what it is to be a person. One contender for a good explanation of personal identity is the "body" theory, which says that a person is to be identified with his or her body. So to be one and the same person across a span of time is just to have one and the same body across that span.

How could the body theory work with someone like Steve Rogers, the original Captain America? Let's call the scrawny kid who hadn't taken the super-soldier serum yet "Stevie," and the athletic (post-serum) man "Steve." Stevie and Steve do not look exactly like each other, nor are they made of exactly the same physical particles. So if the body theory of personal identity required the two bodies to look the same or have all the same particles, then we would say that Stevie and Steve are *not* the same person. But if the theory is more sophisticated, taking into account the normal processes of growth and cell regeneration, a body theory may be able to explain how Stevie and Steve *are* the same person: the former developed into the latter, thus sharing the same body.

Doubts about the body theory come from a thought experiment devised by the philosopher John Locke (1632–1704), in which we imagine people swapping bodies.[1] Suppose one day Steve Rogers and Hank Pym wake up with each other's memories and personalities. They go to the morning Avengers meeting, and the person who looks like Hank Pym starts reminiscing about fighting Nazis in World War II, while the person who looks like Steve Rogers tells a story about his wife, Janet. After careful questioning, everyone realizes what's happened—Rogers and Pym have switched bodies. (Just another day with the Avengers.) So who's who?

If we think the body theory is correct, then we *must* say that the person with Pym's body is Pym and likewise with Rogers. But it seems a bit strange to be forced to say that the person with Pym's body is Pym, even when he has no memory of being Pym. This person behaves and talks as if he is Rogers, and he would deny that he is Pym. These kinds of considerations have led philosophers to other theories, such as ones rooted in collections of psychological attributes like memories and personalities.

I Like You for Your Mind, Honest

Let's call this kind of competitor to the body theory the "psychology" theory. This theory says that some aspect of our psychology is what is essential to us as individuals, so preserving this feature is what preserves personal identity over time.

(Proponents of this kind of theory disagree about *which* psychological feature is key, but that needn't worry us here.) This gives us a better explanation of the body-swapping case of Pym and Rogers, since it predicts that we would think Pym's identity goes with his memories and personality, regardless of which body each ends up in. A difficulty with the psychology theory, though, can be illustrated with a different kind of example.

Suppose Pym invents a duplicating machine that takes a person's brain and splits it into its two hemispheres, then creates two new complete brains out of them—each one identical to the original and retaining all psychological aspects of the original person. Let's say Pym does this to himself and then creates two new bodies to put the new brains in. At the end of it all, we have two new people, each of whom has the same psychological profile as Hank Pym.

Unfortunately, if we think that the psychology theory of personal identity is correct, we have a problem in deciding what we should say about these two new Pym-like men. Is one of them identical to the old Hank Pym? If so, which one? They can't *both* be identical to Pym, since then they would have to be identical to each other. And since there are *two* of them, they are clearly not *one and the same* person. But they both have Pym's psychology, and neither of them appears to have any kind of privileged access—they both have equal claim to it.

The body theory and the psychology theory are two of the main candidates for explaining personal identity, but they are not the only options to choose from. And the difficulties I raised for each of them may not be insurmountable. You may already have some ideas for how we might tweak the body theory to get around the body-swapping problem, or modify the psychology theory to get around the duplication problem. These are fruitful exercises, but let's take what we have discussed here and see how we can use it to discuss superheroes, rather than just "regular" people.[2]

Unmasking the Mantle Theory of Superhero Identity

When we discussed Hank Pym and Steve Rogers, we were talking about them as people, not as their superhero personas. Now let's take up the question we began this chapter with: what can we say about superhero identity that allows us to approach puzzling cases, like the multiple heroic guises of Pym, or the multiple bearers of the Captain America title?

Would it work to simply import a theory of personal identity, such as the body or psychology theory, directly to the case of superheroes? Unfortunately, those theories will not quite capture what we need. Goliath and the Wasp are clearly two different superheroes, but Hank Pym has been both of them at different times. Whatever makes Pym identical to himself over time cannot be the same thing that makes a superhero identical to himself or herself over time; otherwise we would have difficulty saying that Goliath and the Wasp are not identical superhero identities (even though they both may have been assumed by the same person). On the other hand, Captain America is one superhero identity that has been assumed by Steve Rogers (most prominently) and also by others such as John Walker and Bucky Barnes. If Captain America were just a body, or just a certain group of psychological features, it would not be possible for different people (who have different physical and psychological characteristics) to "be" him. But clearly there have been multiple people, all going by the name "Captain America," so we need a new theory of identity.

What should we say about superhero identity if it is not the same thing as personal identity? One possibility would be to draw from the way we talk about superheroes and apply it to the approach we use with personal identity, respecting the fact that it is a different sort of thing to be a superhero than to be a person. Being a superhero is like being a *persona*, or wearing a *mantle*, like when we say, "David Bowie shed the mantle of Ziggy Stardust in the early 1970s, adopting a few years later the persona of the Thin White Duke." Bowie created his personas as a performance artist, and they were something more than just Bowie himself—they were associated with certain features that went beyond the person playing them.

What is it about a mantle that allows for its continuity over a span of time? If it is not just the body or the personality wearing it, what is it that is essential to being a superhero? Two different features stand out when we pose the question this way. One is that a superhero mantle must be of the *appropriate kind*; that is, it must be the mantle of a *superhero*. The second feature is that the bearer of a superhero mantle must have a certain *legitimacy*. Not just anyone can put on a Captain America uniform and actually *be* Captain America; there is a process that must be followed to become certain superheroes. Both of these features—appropriateness and legitimacy—take us beyond the kinds of theories we see for personal identity.

Let's explore these two features in a bit more detail. The aspect of appropriateness of a mantle is just the kind of role that we traditionally associate with superheroes. For one thing, there must be some form of superpower or extraordinary ability associated with it, such as superstrength, lightning speed, extraordinary proficiency with a weapon, and so on. A superhero needs to be extraordinary in some form or other. A superhero must also be a *hero* under some reasonable description, to distinguish superheroes from supervillains. So by "appropriate" I just mean what we would expect—a superhero mantle is one that is associated with some extraordinary ability (or abilities) and some kind of heroism, the reason we call that person a superhero.

The issue of what it is to "legitimately" bear such a mantle is difficult to specify, but we can think of a superhero mantle along the lines of intellectual property. If I invent a new product, I have a legitimate claim to that product, by virtue of the fact that it is my own creation; or if I create some kind of art,

I likewise bear a legitimate claim to that art. The David Bowie example illustrates this point well, because he has the only legitimate claim to his Ziggy Stardust mantle. He could perhaps pass it on to someone else who could give concerts or make albums as Ziggy Stardust, but it would be illegitimate if someone did so without Bowie's blessing (that is, we wouldn't think that such a person would really *be* Ziggy Stardust, as Bowie was). More generally, the legitimacy of a mantle can be traced to its source or pedigree; the person has to have "earned" the mantle, either by creating it or having it bestowed upon him or her by someone in authority (like when Cap gave Kate Bishop the mantle—and bow and arrows—of Hawkeye during one of Clint Barton's "deaths").[3]

Now we have a theory in place—we can call it the "mantle" theory—that will allow us to approach the cases of Hank Pym and Captain America in a bit more detail. Our goal with this theory is to capture the essence of what it is to be a superhero, in the same way the body and psychology theories aim to capture the essence of what it is to be a person. If we can do this successfully, then some of the puzzling cases ought to become less puzzling.

Case Study 1: The Supersoldier

Captain America is one of the most iconic superheroes in the Marvel Universe, and Steve Rogers is the first and most prominent person to wear the patriotic costume. But he is not the only one. In 1987, John Walker took over the job after Steve Rogers quit being Captain America, though Rogers took the job back after a year and a half. Then, in 2007, Steve Rogers allegedly died, disappearing for a few years, leading to his old sidekick Bucky Barnes becoming the new Captain America. When Rogers came back, Bucky continued as Captain America until his apparent death fighting Sin and the Serpent during the "Fear Itself" event, after which Steve once again donned the stars and stripes.[4]

Were John Walker and Bucky Barnes *really* Captain America? Or should we say that they were three different superheroes, all called "Captain America"? According to the mantle view, we have two main things to consider in determining whether they were one and the same superhero: appropriateness and legitimacy. Did each person wear the appropriate mantle, and did they come by it legitimately?

The issue of appropriateness has to do with whether the bearer of the mantle has the right kinds of abilities and whether the bearer is heroic. With Captain America, the abilities are a collection of extraordinary physical features, such as the strength and agility that were given to Rogers through the super-soldier program. (Some proficiency with the round shield is also a key element.) Both Walker and Barnes satisfied these requirements, adding their own unique character to the mantle (Walker was considerably stronger than Rogers, and Bucky carried a gun). They also both acted with an appropriate kind of heroism while they wore the mantle. Neither Walker nor Barnes had a squeaky-clean past, but it is common for heroes to have their unheroic moments. What is important is that while they wear the mantle of a superhero, they are expected to be heroes; repeated failure on this score would put their superhero status in jeopardy.

Legitimacy is the more interesting issue when it comes to considering multiple people being Captain America. For Walker, the moment comes when a government commission, whose job is to manage the "superhuman resources" in America, seeks a replacement for Rogers as Captain America. The government is worried about the bad press they might get from Rogers quitting in an act of protest, so they settle on Walker, another all-American who is making a name for himself as the Super-Patriot, a Cap-esque hero. They offer Walker the role as Captain America and he accepts, while having the following conversation with a member of the commission, Valerie Cooper:

Walker: I couldn't just do the job without changing my name and costume . . . ?

Cooper: No, Captain America is a tradition that goes back decades. We want to preserve it. Well?

Walker: Hmmm . . . Ma'am, if Uncle Sam wanted me to be Mickey Mouse, I'm that kind of American—the kind you can count on. When do I start?[5]

By the end of the issue, Walker is wearing the Captain America costume and everyone is calling him by that name. It seems that now he really *is* Captain America.

For Bucky, we have a different kind of moment, but one that is just as illuminating and decisive. Bucky picked up the available mantle of Captain America in 2008, supported by Tony Stark, who was director of S.H.I.E.L.D. at the time. Then, in 2009, when Rogers came back, he publicly endorsed Bucky as Captain America.[6] So in 2010, the slice of time we are considering for Bucky, Steve Rogers now had a superhero identity similar to that of Nick Fury (a kind of superbureaucrat, with a license to requisition), and Bucky was Captain America. Bucky's legitimacy came first from Stark claiming that Rogers would have wanted Bucky to continue the Captain America legacy, and then from Steve Rogers himself giving him his endorsement.

We see the legitimacy requirement fulfilled in two different ways here—Walker was given the mantle by a government committee (which also took it away from him, giving it back to Rogers), and Barnes was given it by Stark and then Rogers. In the specific circumstances, it makes sense why different mechanisms are legitimate. The mantle of Captain America is sometimes considered to be owned by the government, though it is also in some sense the property of Steve Rogers. And in both the Walker and Barnes cases, viewed in this light, we should be happy to say that people other than Steve Rogers *really were* Captain America.

Case Study 2: Pym Particles

When it comes to Hank Pym, we have a different, and perhaps more subtle, issue concerning the condition of legitimacy. Over the past fifty years, Pym has been Ant-Man, Giant-Man, Goliath, Yellowjacket, and the Wasp, moving back and forth between them from time to time.[7] Is Pym all of these superheroes at once, or just one at a time? How can we evaluate this question? The issue of appropriateness is important, though not the key element to evaluating the situation, so I will discuss that briefly first, and then the subtlety of the legitimacy question at play in Pym's case.

All of these personas are clearly of the appropriate kind to count as superhero mantles. First of all, Pym has been a hero for virtually all of the past five decades, fighting the good fight with the Avengers.[8] Next, it is plausible to think that at most times in his history, Pym has had the ability to perform the superhuman or extraordinary tasks that his identities require. His size-changing abilities are based on the so-called Pym particle, which allows access to another dimension called Kosmos. Pym discovered how to use these particles to send mass to Kosmos (shrinking to ant size) and to draw mass from it (growing to giant size). His other abilities, such as communicating with ants through his Ant-Man helmet, or electrically "stinging" people and flying when he is Yellowjacket, are technological advances that stem from his own abilities as an extraordinary scientist, so it is reasonable to see him as having these abilities any time as well.

The key issue for deciding whether Pym is one superhero at a time, or many at once, is really a conceptual issue linked to the notion of legitimacy. On the mantle view, the question, "Can Pym be multiple superheroes at one time?" becomes the question, "Can Pym legitimately wear multiple superhero mantles at one time?" A similar question arises in issues about personal identity: suppose Pym develops multiple personality disorder, and we ask whether the personalities count as distinct people. According to the body theory of identity, the question, "Is Pym multiple people?" would hinge on whether he has multiple bodies, which he does not; while on the psychology theory it would depend on whether he has multiple sets of psychological features such as memories or personalities, which he may.

How do we decide if Pym can legitimately wear multiple superhero mantles at one time? Think about what it means to wear a mantle or persona. Can David Bowie wear his Ziggy Stardust and his Thin White Duke personas both at the same time? No, certainly not. These personas look and behave totally different. Ziggy is a glammed-out alien, and the Thin White Duke is a classy-looking madman. Aside from the fact that these two personas are radically different, the concept of a persona itself requires us to say that a person can only adopt one at a time. Your persona—however glam or mundane it is—is the face that you put on for the world, and you can only have one face at a time.

A superhero mantle is very much like Bowie's persona, and this limit to one persona at a time transfers to superhero mantles as well. Pym cannot coherently be both Ant-Man and Giant-Man at the same time, for the simple reason that the former is a superhero who shrinks and the latter is a superhero who grows. The prediction of the mantle view that someone can only be one superhero at a time is supported by the way the characters themselves treat the transitions. Even in less clear-cut cases, such as when Pym changes identity from Giant-Man to Goliath (a change mostly only in name and costume), we still see that the superheroes—Pym included—take him to have dropped the Giant-Man persona and picked up the mantle of Goliath.[9]

For example, shortly after Pym becomes Goliath, he ends up stuck at a height of ten feet, which is very unsettling for him. A doctor is called in to give him a checkup, and we have this exchange as the doctor arrives and is let in by Captain America and Quicksilver:

Doctor: I got here as soon as I could, Cap! Where is the patient?

Captain America: Major Carlson! I knew you wouldn't let us down! You'll find this an unusual case! Have you ever heard of . . . Giant-Man?

Doctor: Of course! Then, he's the one I'm to treat?

Quicksilver: He's Giant-Man no longer, Cap! He changed his name to Goliath . . . remember?[10]

Of course, when superheroes change identity, people naturally slip and use old names, but Quicksilver's correction strongly indicates that Giant-Man is gone now, replaced by Goliath.

We also see this when another Avenger, Clint Barton, sheds his Hawkeye identity and becomes Goliath. (At this point, Pym is Yellowjacket, so we don't have two Goliaths at once, though there is to be another Goliath later.) When Barton reveals himself to his fellow Avengers as Goliath after secretly taking Pym's growth serum, Pym asks, "But Hawkeye . . . what of your career as an archer?" Barton answers by snapping his bow in half, after which Pym says, "Then the Avenger called Hawkeye is no more! And, since I've had to swear off the growing thing—looks like there's a new Goliath in our ranks!"[11] As we see, it seems natural to everyone that when Barton picks up the Goliath mantle, he puts down the Hawkeye one. And breaking his bow significantly makes clear that he is not trying to combine two mantles to create a new superhero, a giant archer—he's leaving both mantles as they are and just changing from one to the other.[12]

Are You the Next Goliath?

After seeing how the features of a mantle theory illustrate and explain the interesting cases of people with multiple superhero identities and superheroes played by multiple people, what should we think? Is this the only way to explain superhero identity?

Certainly not, but it does fare better than the theories of personal identity discussed at the beginning. Since superheroes are not just people—they are personas that people adopt—we shouldn't expect a theory of personal identity to neatly fit superheroes. (They have enough trouble fitting normal people!) But by looking at theories of personal identity, we see things that push us toward the kind of discussion we should be having when investigating superhero identity—luckily, we didn't need to talk about superhero costumes, or we'd have to spend an entire book just on Janet van Dyne, the original Wasp![13]

NOTES

1. Locke's example is of a prince's soul or consciousness inhabiting the body of a cobbler, from *An Enquiry Concerning Human Understanding* (1690), book 2, chapter 27, section 15.

2. Two very accessible works on theories of personal identity are John Perry's *A Dialogue on Personal Identity and Immortality* (Indianapolis: Hackett, 1978), and the first chapter of Earl Conee and Ted Sider's *Riddles of Existence: A Guided Tour of Metaphysics* (Oxford: Oxford University Press, 2007).

3. *Young Avengers* #12 (August 2006), reprinted in *Young Avengers: Family Matters* (2007).

4. *Fear Itself* #3–4 (August–September 2011), reprinted in *Fear Itself* (2012). Unbeknownst to Rogers at the time, Bucky was brought back from near death by Nick Fury and later resumed his pre-Cap identity of the Winter Soldier (*Fear Itself* #7.1, January 2012).

5. *Captain America*, vol. 1, #333 (September 1987). Walker's tenure as Cap began here and ran until *Captain America*, vol. 1, #350 (February 1989), and is reprinted in its entirety in *Captain America: The Captain* (2011).

6. Rogers's "death" happened in the landmark *Captain America*, vol. 5, #25 (March 2007), and he came back in the *Captain America Reborn* miniseries (2009–2010). Bucky's run began in *Captain America*, vol. 5, #33 (February 2008), with Rogers endorsing him in *Captain America: Who Will Wear the Shield?* #1 (December 2009).

7. Pym's first appearance as Ant-Man was in *Tales to Astonish*, vol. 1, #35 (September 1962), while Giant-Man first came on the scene in *Tales to Astonish*, vol. 1, #49 (November 1963), both reprinted in *Essential Ant-Man Vol. 1* (2002). Pym's new identity as Goliath appeared first in *Avengers*, vol. 1, #28 (May 1966) and Yellowjacket was born in *Avengers*, vol. 1, #59 (December 1968), reprinted in *Essential Avengers Vol. 2* and *Vol. 3*, respectively (2000 and 2001); and he became the Wasp in *Secret Invasion: Requiem* #1 (January 2009).

8. I say virtually because Pym has had a few mental breakdowns over the years that have led to kidnapping Janet van Dyne (shortly before they get married) in *Avengers*, vol. 1, #59, and to scandalously hitting her in *Avengers*, vol. 1, #213 (November 1981), reprinted in *Secret Invasion: Requiem*.

9. He sometimes uses both shrinking and growing abilities in succession, such as on the recent *Avengers: Earth's Mightiest Heroes* cartoon series. Here he wears the Ant-Man

costume and goes by this name, but he also grows large at times, causing some to refer to him as Ant-Man/Giant-Man. What should we say in this case? At the moment, it seems that Pym is quickly changing from Ant-Man to Giant-Man and back again, too quickly to make a costume change practical. Eventually, if he keeps this up, we should expect him to shed both personas and adopt a new one, consistent with the abilities to both shrink and grow as part of one persona. (He is a genius, after all.)

10. *Avengers*, vol. 1, #29 (June 1966), reprinted in *Essential Avengers Vol. 2*.

11. *Avengers*, vol. 1, #64 (May 1969), reprinted in *Essential Avengers Vol. 3*; for more on Clint Barton's identity crisis, see the chapter by Mark D. White titled "The Way of the Arrow: Hawkeye Meets the Taoist Masters" in this volume.

12. It also seems significant that it is Pym, the person who created the Goliath superhero, who explicitly endorses Barton as being the new Goliath, lending Barton the legitimacy needed to make the transfer successful.

13. I owe many thanks for useful discussions and comments during the writing of this paper to philosophers Roy T. Cook, Peter W. Hanks, Ian Stoner, and Jason Swartwood, and to superhero fans Brandon Bueling, Casey Garske, Sandra Marble, and Matt Nelson.

I AM MADE OF INK:
SHE-HULK AND
METACOMICS

Roy T. Cook

Jennifer Walters, also known as the Sensational (formerly Savage) She-Hulk, is a lawyer, bounty hunter, actress, Avenger, and former member of the Fantastic Four. Jen is one of Marvel Comics' premier superheroines, and better yet, she knows it.

But wait: what is it, exactly, that Jen knows? It isn't merely that she is the most prominent and possibly most powerful female superhero in the (fictional) world that she shares with Spider-Man, Captain America, and her cousin the Incredible Hulk. In addition, Jen *knows* that she is a character in a comic book, and she is able to take advantage of this knowledge in surprising ways. Simply put, Jen is the star of a *metacomic*. By exploring this interesting "superpower" of Jen's, we'll see what her self-awareness says about the nature of comics themselves.

What Is a Metacomic?

To understand the term *metacomics*, it helps to begin at the beginning. Within philosophy, "meta" has at least two distinct but interconnected meanings. The simpler of the two—which sticks rather closely to the original Greek meaning of the term— simply means "beyond" or "about." For example, *metaphysics* involves theorizing about the fundamental nature of reality, a kind of theorizing that goes beyond physics and the other sciences. *Metaethics* involves theorizing about the nature of ethical judgments and ethical practices, rather than merely acting ethically or making particular ethical choices. The term *metahuman*, used to describe characters in comic books who have powers beyond those of ordinary mortals, also falls into this category.

There is another, more specialized use of "meta," however. When it's applied to some term *X*, it roughly means "*X* about *X*." Thus *metadata* are data about data, *metamathematics* is the mathematical study of mathematical systems themselves, and a *metalanguage* is a language used to describe and study other languages. Likewise, a metacomic is a comic that is, in one sense or another, about comics. A metacomic is a type of *metafiction*, which contemporary literary critic Patricia Waugh describes as any "fictional writing which self-consciously and systematically draws attention to its status as an artifact in order to pose questions about the relationship between fiction and reality."[1] Thus a metacomic is any comic that draws attention to some aspect of itself or its creation, where this "meta" aspect of the story is intended not only to propel the story but also to force the reader to think about or question the nature of storytelling itself.

One simple way to turn a comic into a metacomic is to make the protagonist aware that he or she is a character in a comic. This sort of self-awareness is often displayed by "breaking the fourth wall," where the metafictionally self-aware character speaks directly to the audience or to the writers, artists, and editors. In John Byrne's run on *The Sensational She-Hulk*, and (more subtly) in Dan Slott's run on the more recent *She-Hulk*, Jen possesses this sort of self-awareness. Self-aware fourth-wall-breaking does not make Jen unique, though, even among characters in the Marvel Universe. Mutant assassin Deadpool also speaks directly to the audience and is aware that he is a character in a comic book.[2] Jen's abilities are not limited merely to awareness of herself as a fictional character, however. In addition, she is able to use this knowledge to manipulate the comic book world in unique ways.

Why should metafictionally aware Avengers be of interest to philosophers? *Aesthetics*, the philosophical study of the nature of art, has shifted recently from a focus on general questions about art in general[3] to an approach that focuses on the individual arts themselves, including an emphasis on the differences between one art form and another.[4] As a result, it is not surprising that philosophers and other scholars have begun to think about comics and metacomics.[5]

In comparison with most other art forms, comics seem particularly saturated with conventional elements. Thought and speech balloons, textual sound effects, motion lines, and panel borders are all conventional devices that facilitate the representation of sound, motion, time, and space in an artistic medium that consists of silent, static images printed on a two-dimensional page. The better we understand these conventional aspects of comic book storytelling, the better we will be able to appreciate and understand the comics we are reading. The study of metacomics promises to be an extremely valuable tool in this endeavor. After all, what better way to understand how these storytelling conventions function than to see what happens when they are bent, broken, or subverted by the Sensational She-Hulk!

Your Cover Is Blown, Jen

The metafictional madness of John Byrne's run on *The Sensational She-Hulk* begins on the cover of issue #1 (May 1989), which depicts Jen holding a handful of X-Men comics and saying to the comic-shop customer, "Okay, now. This is your second chance. If you don't buy my book this time I'm gonna come to your house and rip up all of your X-Men."[6] Jen is aware that she is the main character of this comic, and is breaking the fourth wall to convince the hesitant buyer to purchase her book. She is also, however, cleverly referring to well-known facts about the comic book industry within the real—that is, *our*—world. She is somehow aware that her previous series, *The Savage She-Hulk*, did not sell well while at the same time X-Men-related comics sold in record numbers. This shows that Jen is not only aware of what happens in her world, but is also quite aware of what happens in ours!

Covers often stray from the literal contents of the comic they enclose, however. Thus if this cover were the only instance of metafictional content in *The Sensational She-Hulk*, it would perhaps not be all that noteworthy. But we don't have to wait long for metafictional content to appear within the comic itself. For example, near the end of issue #1, Jen discovers that the Ringmaster and his Circus of Crime were hired to test the limits of her powers. She then complains, "Some anonymous bad guy is ready to spend three million bucks to find out how tough I am . . . and I know how these things work! It'll be at least my third issue before I find out who it is! Although you readers will probably find out on the next page." And of course we do!

The next two issues also contain metafictional content. On the cover of issue #2 (June 1989), Jen catches up on her cousin Bruce Banner's life by reading issues of *The Incredible Hulk*, playing with the idea that within the Marvel Universe, comic books are historical records of actual events. More interesting, however, is an episode in issue #3 (July 1989), in which Jen regains consciousness after being attacked at the end of issue #2. She initially worries that she has been knocked out for a month, the normal length of time between issues of a monthly comic such as hers. Jen eventually reassures herself that this is not necessarily the case, however, based on the difference between the way time works within a comic (only days or even hours pass between issues) and the way it works in the real world. This knowledge, combined with the fact that her guest star Spider-Man has already appeared (which means that we are halfway into the present issue), allows her to conclude that less than a day has passed since she was knocked out. In short, Jen uses her knowledge of how time is portrayed within comics in order to draw conclusions about what happened while she was unconscious.

"There's a Reader Out There Now!"

This is strange enough, but things get much weirder in issue #4 (August 1989). On page six, Jen has a job interview with the dreamy District Attorney Towers. After the interview, Jen mentions that she wasn't expecting to meet her romantic interest so soon. At this point Towers's assistant, Louise "Weezie" Mason, informs Jen that Towers is married. In the first panel of the next page, Jen asks, "Since when is he married??" and Weezie replies, "Since *now* I suppose. This *is* the first time it's been mentioned." Weezie's response demonstrates that she, like Jen, is aware that she is a character in a comic, but it also reflects a deep insight into the way that truth works in fiction. Although Jen did not meet them, both Weezie and Towers appeared in issues #2 and #3 of the comic. Since Towers's marital status is not mentioned in these earlier issues, at the time they were published there was no fact of the matter regarding whether he was married or not. After all, Byrne could have written a different version of issue #4 where Towers is single and begins a romance with Jen! Weezie is aware that her comments on the previous page made it the case that Towers is married. Further, Weezie presumably does not mean that Towers got married just this minute. Instead, he has been married all along, although the fact that he was married only becomes true (retroactively) as a result of the events in issue #4.

The metafictional weirdness continues in the second panel. Here, Jen shouts out, "What?!? Byrne!! What kind of game are you playing?!?" as she tries to climb out of the panel to physically assault Byrne. Weezie, restraining her, attempts to calm her with the words "Jen!! Control yourself! We're inked and colored! Printed! There's a reader out there now!" There are a number of interesting things going on here, including the continued metafictional self-awareness exhibited by both Weezie and Jen, and the fact that Jen addresses Byrne directly (we have to wait until issue #50 to see Byrne appear in a panel together with Jen, however). This panel also suggests that Jen can *see* Byrne. Normally, we treat panels as a sort of one-way window. We can look through these little rectangles in order to see events within Jen's world, but comic book characters are not meant to be able to look back the other way and see us, much less climb through the panel to assault us!

The most interesting thing in this panel, however, is Weezie's dialogue. Weezie is acknowledging that the printed nature of comics places Towers's marital status not only out of Jen's control but out of Byrne's as well. By the time these events are happening, the comic has been printed, packaged, and purchased by the reader. It's notable that the three things Weezie mentions explicitly—inking, coloring, and printing—are aspects of the creation of the comic that are not under Byrne's direct control as writer and penciller. As a result, there is nothing any of them can do to change things—not even Byrne! Weezie is aware that, in a certain sense, she has no free will, and that her thoughts, statements, and actions for the remaining fifteen pages of issue #4 are already determined, since they are already inked, colored, and printed. Her future has already been laid out and is fixed permanently in ink.

Gutter-Hoppin' and More Amazing Stories

Let's consider the third and fourth panels of this page together, since they are in an important sense a single unit. In the third panel a confused Jen sputters, "But . . . but . . . but," to which Weezie replies, "You're obviously too distraught to go home just yet. C'mon . . . I'll buy you lunch and we can talk." Unlike the previous two panels, there is nothing out of the ordinary in the dialogue here. What is out of the ordinary, however, is how Weezie, dragging Jen along behind her, travels from her office in the third panel to the restaurant in the fourth panel. Weezie crosses this distance in one step, by stepping over the gutter between panels, her right foot touching the floor of the office and her left foot touching the floor of the restaurant. Obviously, the restaurant and the office are not located a mere two or three feet from each other within the fictional world that Jen and Weezie inhabit. But they are located mere fractions of an inch from each other on the page. Here, Weezie and Jen are able to take advantage of the fact that locations far removed from each other within their world are sometimes in close proximity on the page. As a result, it is quicker and more convenient for them to travel across the page than across town.

When Jen and Weezie violate comic book convention by stepping over the gutter, they force us to think about how the transition from one panel to the next operates in standard, non-"meta" comics. We normally make certain assumptions regarding the passage of time and distance when a character is depicted in two different locations in two adjacent panels— an assumption subverted by Weezie and Jen's gutter-jumping mode of transportation. Jen and Weezie's ability to treat the blank space between images as if it were a part of *their* world and not a part of *ours* highlights the critical role that panel transitions, and our assumptions about them, play in our understanding of comics.[7]

In the fifth panel, Weezie begins to explain things to a confused and exasperated Jen. Weezie was formerly the Blonde Phantom, a Golden Age comic book character published by Timely Comics from 1946 to 1949 (*The Blonde Phantom* was a real Golden Age comic, and Timely Comics eventually became Marvel Comics).[8] She eventually retired from crimefighting and married her boss, detective Mark Mason. No longer appearing in a monthly comic, she and her husband began to age. After watching her husband die while other Timely Comics heroes such as Captain America and Namor the Submariner were revived, Weezie decides to manipulate events so that she will appear in Jen's comic book and stop aging.

The strategy works, and Weezie does not get any older. In fact, she even regains her youth in later issues! Weezie is, again, clearly aware of, and able to take advantage of, comic book conventions, including the fact that comic book characters typically do not age. Her presence in *The Sensational She-Hulk* also provides us with an opportunity to reflect on the development of mainstream superhero comics over the last eight decades. A particularly resonant example occurs later in this same issue. After Weezie asks why Jen's clothing doesn't rip in an immodest, inappropriate manner during battles, Jen shows Weezie the Comics Code label sewn into her chemise, reminding us that the industry-imposed self-censorship of the code did not exist when Weezie was appearing in her own comic.

Don't Make the She-Hulk Angry . . .

Later issues of Byrne's run on *The Sensational She-Hulk* contain additional strange metafictional twists and turns. Jen is able to travel between dimensions and is able to reappear after being erased from reality, by tearing the paper on which the comic is printed and stepping through the hole.[9] She is able to recognize regions of deep space by noticing that Byrne has reused background art from an earlier issue.[10] One of the most interesting metafictional stories, however, occurs in Byrne's last issue on the book.

Issue #50 (April 1993) begins with Renee, the editor of *The Sensational She-Hulk*, informing Jen that Byrne has died and that they need to select a new artist for the comic. Jen is then shown a handful of sample pages (depicted as full pages of the comic) in which a number of influential comics creators— Terry Austin, Howard Chaykin, Dave Gibbons, Adam Hughes, Howard Mackie, Frank Miller, Wendy Pini, and Walt Simonson—provide their own distinctive take on the character. Terry Austin's contribution is particularly interesting: an inker who frequently collaborated with Byrne, he depicts Jen and a host of other characters in the style of E. C. Segar's *Thimble Theatre* (Popeye) comic strip, complete with Wimpy, as Galactus, devouring the moon sandwiched within a huge hamburger bun. By depicting Jen and her cohort as *Thimble Theatre* characters, Austin forces us to confront the differences between monthly mainstream superhero comic books and daily newspaper comic strips. In particular, this page highlights the puzzling fact that newspaper comic strips are typically sillier than comic books, yet have traditionally been held in much higher cultural regard than mainstream superhero comics. Issue #50 concludes with Jen discovering Byrne tied up and locked in a closet. When Jen finally reads his new take on the comic—one that renames her Li'l She-Hulk and depicts her and her supporting cast as children—she tosses Byrne out of the window, ironically killing her "creator."

The Sensational She-Hulk only lasted ten issues after Byrne's departure. Jen had to wait until 2004 to star in another solo title, but the wait was worth it. Lasting from 2004 to 2007, Dan Slott's interpretation of the character in *She-Hulk* continued Byrne's metafictional take on the Jade Giantess, although in a subtler vein. In Slott's stories, Jen is able to use comic books bearing the Comics Code seal in the courtroom as legally admissible historical documents.[11] One cover again shows Jen threatening to rip up your favorite comics if you don't buy her book (but this time it's Civil War variants and not X-Men comics).[12] Running through all of this, Jen's new job as a lawyer specializing in defending captured supervillains provides the backdrop for an extended parody of the conceits and conventions of superhero comic book storytelling.

What Are the She-Hulk's Powers?

Reflecting on both Byrne's and Slott's takes on Jen's solo adventures raises more questions. Did the weird, metafictional aspects of the Byrne and Slott stories really happen? If so, does Jen also have these metafictional powers when appearing in *Avengers* comics, and just choose not to use them? Or are Jen's metafictional solo adventures merely imaginary stories, in a similar vein to Marvel's long-running *What If* series of comics? Or perhaps are they merely delusions that Jen and Weezie share?

We can put this question in slightly more precise terms. A work of fiction, such as a novel or comic, can be seen as a partial description of an imaginary or fictional world where things occur as they are depicted within the fiction. Most of the stories published by Marvel Comics intersect and overlap in complicated ways and are meant to be understood as describing a single, very complex fictional world—the Marvel Universe. Jen does not seem to possess any strange metafictional abilities when she appears in *Avengers* or in *Fantastic Four*, however, and in the few comics where she does display these traits either her behavior confuses other, non-"meta" characters, or she is depicted as being a bit crazy.[13]

As a result, there are long-standing disputes regarding whether the She-Hulk stories we have discussed really happened, in the sense that they describe fictional events that occur in the same fictional universe as the events depicted in more traditional Avengers stories, or whether they are descriptions of some other fictional world (perhaps one that Jen imagines or is deluded into thinking she inhabits). As you would guess, the Internet age has only intensified these disagreements. Fortunately, we need not get bogged down in online fan forum discussions, since there is a more authoritative source to which we can turn: the *Official Handbook of the Marvel Universe.*

The original version of the *Official Handbook* was published in 1982, and numerous updated versions and addendums have been published since. The *Official Handbook* consists of detailed biographies and data for major and minor characters in the Marvel Universe, and relevant excerpts from this stand-alone reference work are often included as "bonus material" at the end of trade paperback reprint collections. If, as seems reasonable, we can treat the *Official Handbook* as the definitive source regarding what is and is not the case in the Marvel Universe, then we merely need to look up the entry for Jennifer Walters (actually, she is listed under She-Hulk) and consult the description of her powers and abilities.

Actually, things are not that simple. New editions of the *Official Handbook* do not merely contain additional information that wasn't available in previous editions. Indeed, facts in previous editions can turn out to no longer be facts in later editions through a process called retroactive continuity, or *retconning*, where later stories (often involving time travel or all-powerful cosmic beings) change facts about past stories, or at least our interpretation of them. Jen has been a victim of such retconning. In *Uncanny X-Men* #435 (December 2003), she is depicted as having sex with the Juggernaut, but it is later revealed that this was actually a Jen Walters doppelgänger from a parallel dimension.[14] Nevertheless, while facts about what did or didn't happen in the past might be changed by strange events in the future, resulting in revisions to the *Official Handbook*, presumably changes in what powers a particular character possesses at a particular point in time should not change. Or so one would think.

If we consult the *Official Handbook*, it turns out that even this definitive source is less definitive than we might have hoped. Jen's *Official Handbook* entry included in the May 2002 one-shot *Thing and She-Hulk: The Long Night* states that:

> At one point the She-Hulk and [Weezie] Mason shared the belief that they and those around them were characters in a comic book, but this delusion rarely detracted from the She-Hulk's fighting ability, and she no longer seems to suffer from it.[15]

Several years later, however, the *Official Handbook* entry for Jen included in 2008's *Marvel Encyclopedia: The Avengers* contains the following information about her superpowers:

> She can swap physiques with other humans using Ovoid mind techniques, and seems to have the ability to sense extra-dimensional viewers observing her, a power similar to her cousin's ability to see astral forms; Jen tends to downplay this last trait, as speaking to an unseen audience tends to unsettle those around her.

This later description not only lists Jen's metafictional self-awareness as one of her superpowers, but it also tries to legitimize it as a reasonable superpower within the constraints of the Marvel Universe by comparing it to the Incredible Hulk's ability to perceive supernatural entities.

Maybe Jen's Reading This Chapter Right Now

I won't try to determine definitively whether Jen's metafictional adventures really happened, although it does seem unlikely that a highly delusional woman could successfully balance a legal career and roles in both the Avengers and the Fantastic Four. I will point out, though, that the question is not merely a fan-boyish worry about the details of Marvel continuity (not that there's anything wrong with that!). The puzzle is more far-reaching. If the metafictional aspects of Jen's solo adventures are imaginary or delusional, then this puts the reliability of metafiction, taken as an accurate record of what happens in the fictional world supposedly being described, in doubt. As a result, we will need to reevaluate the role that metafictional content plays in describing the fictional worlds that this sort of fiction purports to describe. Given the increasing frequency and importance of metafiction within comics and other art forms, including literature and film, this promises to have a profound impact on the way that we understand storytelling in general. More important, perhaps, it will have a profound impact on how we understand Jennifer Walters, the Sensational She-Hulk—and perhaps how she understands herself.[16]

NOTES

1. Patricia Waugh, *Metafiction: The Theory and Practice of Self-Conscious Fiction* (London: Routledge, 1982), 2.

2. For a discussion of Deadpool's metafictional adventures, see Joseph J. Darowski, "When You Know You're Just a Comic Book Character," in *X-Men and Philosophy: Astonishing Insight and Uncanny Argument in the Mutant X-Verse*, ed. Rebecca Housel and J. Jeremy Wisnewski (Hoboken, NJ: John Wiley & Sons, 2009), 107–123.

3. For example, the question, "What is it that all artworks have in common that makes them art?"

4. See, for example, Peter Kivy, *Philosophies of Arts: An Essay in Differences* (Cambridge: Cambridge University Press, 1997).

5. See, for example, M. Thomas Inge, *Anything Can Happen in a Comic Book: Centennial Reflections on an Art Form* (Jackson: University Press of Mississippi, 1995), and Roy T. Cook, "Comics Are Not Film: Metacomics and Medium-Specific Conventions," in *The Art of Comics: A Philosophical Approach*, ed. Aaron Meskin and Roy T. Cook (Hoboken, NJ: John Wiley & Sons, 2012).

6. *Sensational She-Hulk* #1 (May 1989), reprinted in *Sensational She-Hulk* (2011), which includes the first eight issues of the series.

7. For an insightful discussion of the role of the gutter in comics, see Scott McCloud, *Understanding Comics: The Invisible Art* (New York: Harper, 1993), ch. 3.

8. *The Blonde Phantom* #12–22 (December 1946–March 1949).

9. *Sensational She-Hulk* #5 (September 1989) and #37 (March 1992).

10. *Sensational She-Hulk* #40 (June 1992).

11. *She-Hulk*, vol. 1, #2 (April 2004), reprinted in *She-Hulk Vol. 1: Single Green Female* (2004).

12. The alternate cover to *She-Hulk*, vol. 2, #8 (May, 2006), reprinted in *She-Hulk Vol. 4: Laws of Attraction* (2007).

13. For example, see *Damage Control*, vol. 2, #3 (January 1990).

14. *She-Hulk*, vol. 2, #21 (September 2007), reprinted in *She-Hulk Vol. 5: Planet Without a Hulk* (2007).

15. *Thing and She-Hulk: The Long Night* one-shot (May 2002), reprinted in *The Thing: Freakshow* (2005).

16. Thanks go to Rob Callahan, Alice Leber-Cook, Stephen Nelson, and an audience at the University of Minnesota–Morris for helpful feedback on this material.

THE SELF-CORRUPTION
OF NORMAN OSBORN:
A CAUTIONARY TALE

Robert Powell

It was arguably the gravest existential threat in the Marvel Universe: the Skrulls had launched one of the most sophisticated campaigns to fulfill their religious prophecy of conquering Earth. Using their shape-shifting abilities, they infiltrated our heroes' world by replacing iconic and trusted heroes in preparation for a full-scale invasion. The ensuing battle for Earth would shape the status quo of the Marvel Universe for years to come.

One of the many crippling effects of the Skrull invasion— aside from the broken bonds of trust and solidarity among the world's heroes—was the complete failure and corruption of Earth's protective institutions. In the aftermath of the Skrull invasion, S.H.I.E.L.D. was dismantled and Norman Osborn, the former Green Goblin, was given "the keys to the kingdom": directorship over national security. He immediately transformed

S.H.I.E.L.D. into H.A.M.M.E.R., consolidated an evil cabal of Machiavellian villains, and assembled his own Avengers team—the Dark Avengers—made up of replacements for real heroes like Wolverine and Spider-Man. As we'll see in this chapter, Osborn's "Dark Reign" is a cautionary tale with a philosophical lesson.

Osborn's Oratory and the Dark Reign

Osborn's rise to power mirrors some specific themes in Plato's (429–347 BCE) dialogues featuring Socrates (469–399 BCE), his teacher, and Gorgias (485–380 BCE), an Athenian orator. Gorgias was one of the earliest *Sophists*, who developed a school of rhetoric concerned with persuasion, and whom Socrates criticized for neglecting the intrinsic value of truth in favor of the pursuit of self-interest.

Socrates makes a critical distinction between *craft* (or art) and *knack*. The former is a genuine endeavor designed to produce something of value, whereas the latter is a mere simulation of a craft. Acts of sophistry, such as Gorgias's rhetoric, corrupt the individual by limiting their capabilities to reach for the truth, and corrupt society by substituting a flimsy substitute for a true endeavor. Gorgias's protégé Polus vehemently defends the sophistic enterprise, claiming that anyone would envy and admire Sophists with the power of persuasion that enabled them to imprison whomever they please and confiscate property. In Polus's eyes, such a character represents the ideal Sophist and proves the value of this "art." Socrates holds firm, however, noting that such Sophists are to be pitied rather than admired since they have no control over themselves and ultimately no power at all.

Norman Osborn has much in common with Polus's ideal Sophist. He not only uses his newfound position to further his own well-being at the cost of society at large, but he does so by subverting established heroic institutions like S.H.I.E.L.D.

and the Avengers, substituting a facsimile for the "real thing." Furthermore, both during and after the Skrull invasion, Osborn proves himself to be quite media savvy, favoring strategic use of rhetoric to disguise truth. His defense of the national capital is well timed and documented, and his shot that takes out the Skrull Queen is captured on camera minutes after Tony Stark has been observed leaving the battle scene to repair his suit—both of which secure Osborn's rise to the head of H.A.M.M.E.R.[1] It is noteworthy that, in keeping with the sophistic paradigm, it is never revealed throughout the entire Dark Reign what H.A.M.M.E.R. actually means. Nevertheless it carries the image of an organization responding to widespread anxiety and insecurity, and one that will stop at nothing in the name of security.

Osborn's first recruit to H.A.M.M.E.R. is Victoria Hand, a woman known in the highest ranks of S.H.I.E.L.D. for her criticism of Nick Fury's "soft" policies. Hand is offered the position of deputy director and is given her first assignment by Osborn:

> I want to weed out the malcontents. I want an army of men and women ready to take back the world. And those who are not ready will be replaced. I want a full report on the fifty state initiative . . . I want you to take this Starktech Golden Goose of a Helicarrier and I want it scrapped . . . You use my designs. You put them into full production. I want this red and gold out of sight.[2]

Osborn plans to make his mark on the world in a territorial manner, vigilantly and jealously safeguarding his "kingdom" against any who dare to oppose him. To this end, he also assembles his Dark Avengers, including many villains placed in the roles of Avengers (such as Bullseye posing as Hawkeye) and some particularly volatile and unbalanced Avengers (such as Ares and the Sentry, respectively). Last and true to form,

Osborn adapts some leftover Stark armor in a red, white, and blue motif, and christens himself the Iron Patriot.

The Split Osborn Identity

Osborn's heavy reliance and perhaps dependence on the media creates a hollow simulacrum that he has trapped himself into maintaining while forgoing any form of self-cultivation. It is important to recall that his rise to power involved the theft of information or equipment from other heroes. In fact, much of his strategy in rising to power involved manipulating or corrupting structures that were already in place. In this regard, Osborn's intentions and behavior mirror those of Alcibiades in Plato's dialogue *Alcibiades*, which focuses on the importance of authenticity.

Alcibiades is a young and arrogant Athenian noble who is shocked to discover, after his discussions with Socrates, that he knows very little about justice. With a well-crafted series of questions, Socrates reveals Alcibiades's complete ignorance of the root concepts of things he wishes to speak authoritatively on in public. Socrates attempts to nudge Alcibiades in a more virtuous direction, warning that his greed and thirst for fame are misplaced and result from his lack of self-awareness. Alcibiades compares himself to and competes with his fellow officials in Athens. In response, Socrates points out that Alcibiades is actually harming himself and neglecting the problems facing the city. He tells him that one can only grow through critical self-reflection, typically with a friend who looks out for one's best interest and will not fall prey to flattery.[3]

Osborn lacks the insight Socrates imparts to Alcibiades, and serves as a cautionary tale. Like Alcibiades, Osborn seeks to impose his influence anywhere he can, at the expense of more socially beneficial and cooperative options. He approaches his new role with all of his personal vendettas at the fore and yet masked under cover of national security. For instance, in the aftermath of the Utopia event, Osborn seeks personal revenge on Namor by slaughtering Atlanteans in the name of national security.[4] Unfortunately, no one cautions him as Socrates cautioned Alcibiades. Rather than cultivate the company of true friends who will keep him in line, Osborn surrounds himself mostly with fellow villains, who will not criticize his goals and actions and are poised to take advantage of his impending failure.

On the surface, Osborn appears to be a sane and stalwart civil servant, but beneath he is just as monstrous as his alternate persona, the Green Goblin. In this way he is like Robert Reynolds, the Sentry, who has a second personality called the Void. For Reynolds (as in physics), for every action there is an equal and opposite reaction; any act of good performed by the Sentry results in a commensurate act of malfeasance by the Void.[5] An amplified version of the super-soldier serum that created Captain America gave Reynolds the "power of one million exploding suns" but also created the persona of the Void, with whom he struggled for years to maintain control over his powers. It is revealed late in the Dark Avengers series that Osborn offered to "help" Reynolds by giving him a new formula, one that actually gave the Void control of the Sentry.[6] It is appropriate that Osborn chooses to corrupt the Sentry, a man whose affliction mirrors his own. Osborn often struggles with the Green Goblin for control of his mind, particularly during times of stress.

During their early missions, Osborn assured Reynolds that there is no Void, but when Reynolds expresses hesitation at slaughtering Atlantean terrorists, Norman tells him, "You don't have to do anything, Bob . . . We need him for this. We need the hand of God to smite these bastards to hell."[7] It is no accident that Osborn plays with Reynolds's mind while absolving him of responsibility for the Void's actions. After learning that the heroic Noh-Varr, his Captain Marvel, has left his Avengers team, Osborn retreats to his private quarters, where he does battle with his Goblin persona: "N-n-no . . . I'm in charge. Me. Not you. Me. I'm in charge," to which the Goblin answers, "Oh Norman . . . Norman, Norman, stop kidding yourself. I'm here, I'm always here."[8] By releasing the Sentry's evil side, Osborn may be clearing the way to let the Goblin take over as well, absolving himself of any responsibility for what he does afterward.

Wag the Goblin

> You pull this off . . . you are bulletproof. Untouchable.
> It will take the leaders of the free world decades to
> come to grips with what you've accomplished.
>
> —Loki[9]

With his Avengers team, and an image of himself as a stalwart hero protecting his country, the only thing missing from the Osborn equation is an inauthentic war. Everything has come full circle when Loki—disguising himself as the Green Goblin persona—goads a mentally weak Osborn into launching an attack on Asgard without presidential sanction.

The Siege of Asgard is the ultimate monument to Norman Osborn's sophistry, because he purposefully puts the country in danger in the name of national security. In order to appear successful in his duty of securing the nation, he chooses to actively endanger it, creating the problem to which he can provide the solution. Significantly, there are no institutional safeguards in place to prevent him from doing so, a fact driven home when we see the White House crafting its response to the Siege. Fully aware of Osborn's insubordination, the president questions his staff regarding their options.[10] One of his staffers laments that ordinarily they would call the Avengers in such an event, but ironically they are under Osborn's command.

Before the Siege begins, the Sentry's wife, Lindy, reveals how her husband was a narcotics addict before the serum made him into the Sentry:

> Instead of drugs . . . it became about power. He was addicted to the Sentry. And he had just as much control over that as he did the other. So that answers the question right? Who is the Sentry? Who is the Void? It's what happens when someone who doesn't deserve power gets power.[11]

Lindy's analysis and judgment of Reynolds holds for Osborn and the rest of his Avengers as well, putting the Siege of Asgard into perspective and highlighting why things go as disastrously as they do. After interrogating the Void, Osborn learns that Lindy is the last remaining source of Reynolds's conscious control. In order to protect his most prized weapon, Osborn has Bullseye (his fake Hawkeye) indulge his murderous instincts by killing Lindy.[12] With all of his weapons primed, Osborn proceeds with his Siege, ultimately destroying the city of Asgard with a raging Void-controlled Sentry.

During the Siege, Ares learns that Osborn has manipulated him into leading the assault against his fellow gods. He is shocked and angered when Heimdall, the Asgardian who sees all in the nine realms, informs him that he was not saving Asgard from Loki's madness, but rather aiding him.[13] In response to his mutiny, the Void literally rips Ares in two, which is broadcast live on television and seen by Ares's son Phobos (one of Nick Fury's Secret Warriors). In retaliation, the young god attacks the White House. Unable to confront the president personally, Phobos leaves a note chastising him for the choices he made that led to the current situation with Osborn:

> Dear Mortal head of state, I came here today to explain to you the true and total consequences of your actions over the last several months. . . . Surely, fortune favors

you and the men I spared enjoy it. But before you wash your hands of my father's blood I would encourage you to reflect on what brought us to this point. You sacrificed honor for expediency. You traded intent for quick action. You were wrong and we all suffered for it.[14]

Phobos's letter speaks not only to the president of the United States but also to the wider system that allowed individuals who did not deserve power and were unfit for it to acquire it. It is also fitting that the Siege provides an opportunity for the heroes of the old guard to put aside their past differences and work together at a critical moment, ending the Dark Reign and ushering in a Heroic Age.

Hoist by His Own Petard

Ultimately, Osborn—the proverbial Alcibiades and Sophist—is defeated by his own avarice when he is betrayed by the very institutions he created (such as the Dark Avengers and the evil Cabal) to secure power. His lack of self-control and destructive addiction to power mirror the Sentry's, and it is fitting that he is publicly revealed to be under the influence of the Green Goblin after the Void is revealed to be in control of the Sentry.

Osborn could have become a hero if he had reined in his passions and committed himself to a genuine integration and development of his character. Sadly, he had few honest peers like Victoria Hand in his regime, and his opportunities for critical self-reflection were few and far between. When incarcerated after the Siege, he reveals some rationale for carrying out his duty in the manner in which he did, but it is a distorted rationalization driven by an exaggerated appreciation of the dangers in the Marvel Universe.[15] Osborn's Achilles' heel is his insecurity, which led him to react rashly to diverse and independent sources of power. Instead of integrating and understanding potential and powerful sources of power, he attempted to undercut, possess, and subvert them. Ultimately his ambitions and insecurities eclipsed all of his heroic potential. He had the great power, but he never embraced the great responsibility that came with it—especially to himself.

NOTES

1. *Thunderbolts* #125 (December 2008), reprinted in *Thunderbolts Vol. 3: Secret Invasion* (2009), and *Secret Invasion* #8 (January 2009), reprinted in *Secret Invasion* (2009). For more on Osborn's manipulation of the public trust in the Avengers, see the chapter titled "Shining the Light on the Dark Avengers" by Sarah Donovan and Nick Richardson in this volume.

2. *Dark Avengers* #1 (March 2009); the entire series was collected in the hardcover *Dark Avengers* (2011).

3. *Alcibiades*, in Plato, *Complete Works*, ed. John M. Cooper (Indianapolis: Hackett, 1997), 132e–135e. Standard pagination is given whenever Plato is quoted, so you can find the relevant passages in any reputable translation.

4. *Dark Reign: The List—X-Men* (November 2009), reprinted in *Dark Reign: The List* (2010).

5. *Sentry* #1–5 (2000–2001), reprinted in *The Sentry* (2005).

6. *Dark Avengers* #13 (March 2010).

7. *Dark Avengers* #6 (August 2009).

8. Ibid.

9. *Siege: Loki* #1 (June 2010), reprinted in *Siege: Battlefield* (2010).

10. *Siege* #1 (March 2010), reprinted in *Siege* (2010).

11. *Dark Avengers* #13.

12. *Dark Avengers* #14 (April 2010).

13. *Siege* #2 (April 2010), reprinted in *Siege*.

14. *Siege: Secret Warriors* #1 (June 2010), reprinted in *Siege: Battlefield*.

15. *Dark Avengers* #16 (July 2010) and *Osborn* #1–5 (January–June 2011, reprinted in *Osborn: Evil Incarcerated*, 2011).

PART THREE

SHOULD THE AVENGERS DO MORE THAN AVENGE?

FORGIVERS ASSEMBLE!

Daniel P. Malloy

The very first comic book I ever bought was an issue of *West Coast Avengers*, a long-running spinoff of the main *Avengers* book. I don't remember what it was about or which issue it was. I only remember three things: it cost me 75 cents (!), it ended in a cliffhanger of some kind—and it had a really cool cover, which is why I bought it. The cover featured this great drawing of some guy dressed in purple and sporting a bow and arrow. I didn't realize it then, or even after I'd read the book (many many times), but that guy on the cover was a villain. Not in that comic, of course, by which time he was a well-established hero, but much earlier in his purple-clad career. Years later I found out that the character whose design and weaponry had gotten me interested in comic books—Clint Barton, the hero named Hawkeye—had actually started his life as a villain.

Hawkeye isn't the only former villain among the Avengers' ranks. Several other high-profile team members over the years—the Scarlet Witch, Quicksilver, Vision, Wonder Man, and the Black Widow, to name a few—began life on the wrong side of the law. Certainly other superhero teams have recruited from the ranks of their enemies, but not quite as often or as prominently as the Avengers have. This remarkable fact gives us a chance to explore two of the most fascinating yet troublesome topics in moral philosophy—forgiveness and redemption—issues that must be dealt with together. Without forgiveness there can be no redemption, and forgiveness that does not grant redemption is hollow.

Time Travel, Retcons, and Forgiveness

In the universe of comic books, unlike the real world, it's possible to change the past. Sometimes heroes or villains go back in time to change or preserve the course of history—that's Kang the Conqueror's modus operandi. More often, writers decide that something happened in the past that they failed to mention or that their characters didn't know about, so they fill in the gaps, not changing history as much as completing it (after the fact). In the most extreme cases, the writers judge that the history of their characters doesn't work anymore, for some reason, so they just make up a new one. Fans—often in a critical tone—call this process a *retcon*, short for retroactive continuity, changing past stories to make them consistent with present ones. This fantastic ability possessed by comics creators is one of the reasons very few heroes and villains in comics ever stay dead—if writers can't find a way to bring them back to life in current stories, they change earlier ones so they didn't actually die.

Unfortunately, we in the real world are pretty much stuck with the past as it is. Oh, we can deny it or lie about it, but we can't actually change past events—what has happened has happened, and that's the way it always will be. This is what philosopher Hannah Arendt (1906–1975) called the "predicament of irreversibility."[1] Once an event has occurred or an action has been taken, there is no going back. This predicament affects us most personally when the thing we would like to reverse is some action of our own or one that has affected us. Who wouldn't want to go back and retract those hurtful words or get in that one great comeback that you only thought of after you'd left the party? Who wouldn't want to avoid getting mugged or being betrayed? We can't do it, though. The best we can do is manage how we feel about that event.

Because we're talking about forgiveness, let's focus on a case where one person has harmed another—or, at least, where one person feels they've been harmed by another. Consider Simon Williams, the Avenger known as Wonder Man and originally, like Hawkeye, a villain. With the help of the villain Baron Zemo, Simon was exposed to "ionic energy" and acquired superpowers in an attempt to exact revenge upon Tony Stark (otherwise known as Iron Man). Stark Industries was in direct competition with Williams Innovations, which Simon's family owned. Stark did not compete with Williams unfairly— he simply offered better products or cheaper prices or some combination thereof. Nevertheless, Williams believed he had been wronged by Stark, and became Wonder Man to seek revenge.[2]

There are several ways we can deal with being wronged, but they all start from a basic, perhaps even instinctual reaction: resentment. Resentment is not a bad thing in itself. In fact, it is arguably an important part of self-preservation—at least according to philosopher and theologian Bishop Joseph Butler (1692–1752). In Butler's sermons on resentment and forgiveness, he argues that resentment should not be looked on as a moral failing. It is simply a necessary reaction to being harmed or wronged, and teaches us to avoid similar situations in the future.[3] It can, however, become a moral failing if we allow excessive resentment to control our actions, as is the case with Wonder Man. Excessive resentment leads to revenge— and the antidote to it is forgiveness.

Butler's arguments for the link between forgiveness and resentment have been taken as gospel (pun intended—please forgive me) by most contemporary philosophers who think about forgiveness, although they also typically argue that Butler's definition is correct but incomplete. For instance, excuses pose a particular problem for Butler's account. By excuses I don't mean the classics like "the dog ate my homework" or "I have a headache." In this context, an excuse is a reason for having acted or failed to act that mitigates or eliminates moral (or legal) responsibility.[4] For instance, since the Vision was an artificial "synthezoid" created and programmed by Ultron to destroy the Avengers, he was arguably not responsible for those actions, so he has an excuse in our sense.[5] The problem with excuses as far as Butler's account of forgiveness is concerned is that they too suppress or reduce resentment, but in a completely different way. We have to add to Butler's account that forgiveness does not deny the wrongdoer's responsibility for his or her actions.

At the same time, forgiveness, like excuses, maintains an aura of disapproval. When I forgive someone, I must maintain that the action for which I am forgiving them was wrong to begin with. It is not made right by my forgiveness—forgiveness does not condone an action. This may seem a fairly obvious point, but that does not prevent people from getting confused about it. For instance, take the case of the second modern Black Knight, Dane Whitman. Attempting to prove his worth to the Avengers and atone for the misdeeds of his uncle (his villainous predecessor as the Black Knight), Dane infiltrates and then betrays the second incarnation of the Masters of Evil.[6] Now, in all likelihood, Dane had to do some pretty unsavory things to join the group—they are the Masters of *Evil*, after all. At the very least, we know that Dane had to lie to his fellow Masters of Evil. These deeds, however, do not need to be forgiven. We would condone them; whatever evil Dane did was ultimately in the interest of preventing even greater evil by the Masters of . . . well, you know.

Can Cap Forgive the Rest of His Kooky Quartet?

So, forgiveness is the act of giving up resentment against a wrongdoer without denying his responsibility for doing wrong (as excusing him would) or the wrongness of the wrong (as condoning it would). There are (at least) two reasons for offering forgiveness. First, forgiveness benefits the one who forgives, because to hold on to resentment is to allow the wrongdoer more power over oneself than he deserves. Second, by forgiving wrongdoers, we make reconciliation between ourselves and them possible. Offering forgiveness is a step toward reestablishing a relationship between the wrongdoer and the person wronged. This is why answering the question in the title of this section—"Can Cap forgive the rest of his Kooky Quartet?"—is tricky but essential to understanding the infamous second lineup of the Avengers, as well as forgiveness itself.

In issue #16 of *Avengers* (vol. 1, May 1965), the founding members of the team decide that they need to take a break. They are not disbanding the team or leaving the team altogether—they simply need some time off (after a grueling first fifteen issues). So they look for replacements, and they find them rather quickly in the form of three reformed *supervillains*: Hawkeye, Quicksilver, and the Scarlet Witch. Previously, Hawkeye had been a minor foe of Iron Man (under the sway of the Black Widow, no less, also a villain at the time), and Quicksilver and the Scarlet Witch had been members of (their father) Magneto's original Brotherhood of Evil Mutants (note the word "evil"). Together with honorary founding member Captain America (whom the "real" founding members thawed out from a block of ice in the fourth issue of the series), these baddies-turned-goodies became the new Avengers lineup.

(handwritten margin note: # Naming or Cuss Words)

The problem with Cap's Kooky Quartet, as this incarnation of the Avengers came to be known, is that they somehow became heroes "overnight." In hindsight, several decades and hundreds of stories later, there's no doubt that they were sincere, although Quicksilver is still an arrogant, hotheaded jerk, Hawkeye—well, he's an arrogant, hotheaded jerk too—and the Scarlet Witch, well, she has her own issues that we'll talk about later. (In contrast, Cap just died a few times, but he's better now.) Nonetheless, we should still be concerned about the fact that these three have performed evil deeds. A villain can't simply say, "Oh, uh, look, I've thought it over, and well, I'm a good guy now." Evil deeds don't disappear when one has a change of heart, nor do they vanish when just anybody says it's okay. In this case, it's appropriate that it was Iron Man who introduced the new Avengers lineup, because Hawkeye's entire criminal career basically consisted of trying to defeat him. So Iron Man has what contemporary philosopher Claudia Card calls the "moral power" to forgive Hawkeye: as a victim of Hawkeye's crimes, Shellhead has the authority to grant absolution and forgiveness.[7]

Who Will Forgive the Mutants?

But Quicksilver and the Scarlet Witch—mutant siblings Pietro and Wanda Maximoff—pose more of a problem. To be sure, there are mitigating factors in their case: for example, they only joined the Brotherhood of Evil Mutants to repay a debt to Magneto for saving Wanda's life from an anti-mutant mob.[8] To show their gratitude, Wanda and Pietro swore their allegiance to Magneto's pro-mutant cause, and went on to become supervillains. When they decided their debt had been paid they left Magneto's service, and later (naturally) they turned up on the Avengers' doorstep, ready to serve. They did, however, commit crimes while with Magneto, albeit reluctantly, and they were never punished. So we have to assume that their crimes were forgiven or excused. By whom, though? The only people with any obvious power to forgive or excuse are the victims, and we never see or hear anything from them. Without that, there is no way to say that forgiveness has been granted.

There are unusual cases, however, where forgiveness can be granted without the victim's assent. For instance, suppose Pietro and Wanda had, in the course of their careers as supervillains, accidentally caused the death of a security guard named Stanley. Obviously, in the case of death, the victim can't forgive or excuse what happened. If Stanley is not available to forgive Pietro and Wanda, who can? Perhaps nobody, in which case theirs will be an evil deed that is forever on their heads. But maybe the security guard had a wife. This, of course, makes their crime worse, but there is a bright side. Stanley's wife is a victim of the Maximoffs' crime also, and as such, she has the right to speak not only on her own behalf, but on her husband's as well. She can, if she chooses, grant Pietro and Wanda forgiveness.

That's a fairly uncomplicated case of what we call *third-party forgiveness*. Things become much more complicated when the third party is not a direct or indirect victim of the crime, as when the Avengers grant Quicksilver and the Scarlet Witch a sort of absolution by allowing them to join the team. To see why this is a problem, think back to Bishop Butler's analysis, in which forgiveness is forgoing revenge and overcoming resentment. A third party who isn't injured by the evil deed has no reason to feel resentment and no motive for revenge. Therefore, it would seem that there can be no such thing as third-party forgiveness, and the Avengers, even Cap, cannot absolve Quicksilver and the Scarlet Witch of their crimes.

That understanding of forgiveness, however, takes a rather narrow view of what it is to be injured by a crime. A crime is a violation of a law, and our duty to obey laws, moral or otherwise, does not depend solely on our relationship to any random person we may harm by not obeying them. This duty is owed to the community more generally—that is why we can be punished for crimes that have no specific victim. When I jaywalk, for instance, I am not harming anyone—I'm just crossing the street in an illegal way. In fact, the only person likely to suffer any bodily harm from my habit of ignoring crosswalks is me (if it weren't for my Herculean frame, that is). Nonetheless, by ignoring the laws about when and where I may cross streets, I am causing harm to the community as a whole: I am disrupting the orderly flow of traffic and the overall harmony of the community. Admittedly, others are probably disrupting it more: arsonists, kidnappers, and mimes, as well as supervillains (and mimes), all come to mind as excellent examples of disruptive influences in a community. But my jaywalking is also disruptive—just not to the same degree (especially compared to mimes).

Since the community as a whole is being injured by a crime (which, you will note, rhymes with mime), the community would seem to have the moral power to forgive, at least in the absence of a direct victim. And the Avengers are representatives, in a way, of the community, so it follows that they do have some right to forgive Wanda and Pietro for their crimes. Notice, though, that this right of the community takes a backseat to the rights of the victims themselves. If the victims are in a position where they are capable of offering forgiveness (that is, they are neither dead nor comatose, still in possession of their faculties, and are not practicing mimes) and refuse to do so, the community must respect that (to some degree). There are cases where a refusal to forgive would be utterly unreasonable, and ones where arguably forgiveness should never be offered. (Here's a hint: *mimes*.)

Forgive Me!

Once we know who does and does not have the right to forgive a crime, the next question is, when *should* someone forgive a crime? This question may be the trickiest of the bunch.

There are actually two sides to it: first, what sorts of crimes can be forgiven and under what circumstances, and second, whether there are crimes that are simply unforgivable.

In thinking about the first problem, we have to realize that while victims of a crime have a right to forgive, they have no obligation. Only the victim can decide when and if a crime should be forgiven. Still, it's possible to establish some broad guidelines about forgiveness. A person shouldn't be too quick or too slow to forgive. Forgiving too quickly displays a lack of self-respect, while being too reluctant to forgive manifests a grudging resentment. In each case, the victim of the crime is granting too much power over themselves to the perpetrator. The victim who forgives instantly is almost agreeing with the perpetrator that the victim was worth little enough to justify the crime. The person who forgives too slowly, or refuses to forgive altogether, remains forever defined as the victim of another.[9]

In deciding what should be forgiven and when, we need to consider not just the victim but the perpetrator as well. We often hear reformed villains speak about "earning forgiveness," but this notion is false. To earn something is to acquire a right to it, and there is no right to be forgiven. Such a right would imply an obligation on the part of the victim to forgive, and that right simply doesn't exist. However, by displaying remorse, performing acts of repentance, or making reparations, a perpetrator can make it more reasonable for a victim to forgive, even to the point where it seems unreasonable to withhold forgiveness.

Take Hawkeye, for instance: in his criminal days he harmed Tony Stark, so Stark has the right to forgive him—something he does quite quickly (perhaps too quickly). But suppose Stark had not been so quick to forgive—at what point would his refusal have become unreasonable? There is no clear answer, but in Hawkeye's case, he clearly repented of his earlier criminal behavior and changed his ways, making him a likely candidate for forgiveness. Once he's helped to save the world once or twice, he becomes still more likely. Once he's saved Tony's own armor-clad bacon a few more times, it seems that Tony would be unreasonable if he still resented Hawkeye's earlier actions.[10]

Hawkeye is a fairly easy case (if there is such a thing as an "easy" case of forgiveness). Suppose we look at something a little more difficult—what if the perpetrator of the crime is unrepentant? Could, for example, Cap forgive the Red Skull, or the Fantastic Four forgive Doctor Doom?[11] From what we've already said, the answer is yes, of course they *could*, so the real question is whether they *should*. The answer seems to be no, unless they have good reason to believe that such forgiveness might actually spur the villain in question to become repentant. Part of the purpose of forgiveness is to reestablish harmonious relations. If the perpetrator is unrepentant and likely to remain so, then forgiveness will fail in this purpose. On the other hand, if the perpetrator has admitted wrongdoing and expressed remorse for it, or seems likely to do so given the right encouragement, then forgiveness can serve this purpose. To forgive the Red Skull or Doctor Doom, given their immense pride in their criminal actions (as well as their refusal to admit any wrongdoing, thinking themselves righteous and noble), would be equivalent to condoning their actions. But to forgive someone on the verge of repenting his or her actions might be the last bit of encouragement needed to start reforming them.

Forgiveness in the House of M

We've discussed guidelines for forgiveness in terms of the people involved in a crime, the victims and perpetrators, but we've neglected the issue of the crime itself. It's one thing for Hawkeye to make amends for his attacks on Iron Man, but it's quite another for the Wasp to forgive her husband, Hank Pym, for hitting her, or for the Marvel Universe to forgive the

Scarlet Witch for warping reality itself.[12] There are various degrees of crimes to consider, some of which are more easily forgiven than others. There are also a variety of factors to be considered, including the severity of the harm and the number of people impacted by a particular crime. To cut to the chase, though, let's consider whether there are any crimes that simply ought not to be forgiven, ever.

As we consider the possibility of an unforgivable crime, we can take one of two approaches. The first claims that certain crimes are unforgivable by their very nature: there is something inherent in the crime itself that makes forgiveness unthinkable. For instance, we could argue that Hank Pym's abuse of his wife was unforgivable, not because of the actual physical harm he inflicted, but because of the violation of their relationship that it represented. By that logic, Janet van Dyne should never have forgiven Hank, or was at least behaving unreasonably when she did. Also, some stories hint that the Scarlet Witch may have been molested as a child.[13] If it is true that Wanda was molested as a child, forgiveness for the perpetrator may simply be out of the question; that crime itself is too terrible to forgive, regardless of any circumstances in any particular instance of it.

The other approach to unforgivable crimes maintains that there is no crime that is unforgivable by its nature, but there are some crimes that are unforgivable depending on their degree. For example, a single murder might be forgivable, but attempted genocide would not be. We can look again to the Scarlet Witch: in the *House of M* miniseries (2005), Wanda used her reality-warping powers to, well, warp reality, but this time on a grand scale. She attempted to grant every hero his or her fondest wish. In theory, that sounds great, but in actuality, it meant forcing the entire world to live a lie, one that robbed each and every person of their individual histories and identities. There are some mitigating factors: Wanda was in the middle of a breakdown and perhaps not entirely responsible for her actions. If we accept that, then there is no crime to be forgiven, because it is excused. If, however, the reality-warping was voluntary and intentional, with no excuse available, then we might have an unforgivable crime.

These two approaches are usually combined, which brings to mind the contributions of Wanda's brother, Quicksilver, to this whole reality-warping business. In the latter stages of *House of M*, it is revealed that it was actually Pietro who caused the whole mess—albeit with the best of intentions. With Wanda's reality-warping powers expanding and her sanity collapsing, many of the world's heroes gathered to decide what should be done about her. When Pietro heard someone suggest killing Wanda to save the world, he went to his sister and suggested the bit of reality-warping that began the whole story line. In doing this, Pietro arguably performed both sorts of unforgivable crime. On the one hand, he was indirectly responsible for the warping of reality on the largest scale imaginable, and on the other, he manipulated his mentally unstable sister to achieve it.

The Paradox of Forgiveness

To be sure, not everyone accepts that there is such a thing as an unforgivable crime. French philosopher Jacques Derrida (1930–2004) argued that if forgiveness is to have any meaning, it must be granted to the (seemingly) unforgivable.[14] Forgiving the forgivable is (relatively) easy, and comes with benefits; by forgiving a repentant and remorseful friend, for instance, we repair the friendship, generating a type of exchange. But forgiving the unforgivable is the only kind of "pure" forgiveness (similar to "pure" altruism), where there can be no expectation of reward. To forgive that which cannot be forgiven is to forgive without hope, or need, or want. If this is how we understand forgiveness and the unforgivable, then the crimes we have examined so far have not been unforgivable. In each case, those who would be called on to forgive have the possibility of establishing or reestablishing a relationship with the forgiven person. In order to find an unforgivable crime, by Derrida's logic, we don't need a particular kind of crime, but a particular kind of criminal: namely, an unrepentant one. Or to make the situation perfect, a deceased unrepentant criminal would be ideal—there is then no hope of the forgiven criminal having a change of heart.

Derrida's discussion of the forgivable expresses what some have called the *paradox of forgiveness* though it is really the paradox of forgiveness and repentance. The paradox runs something like this: you can't forgive an unrepentant criminal, because then you are simply excusing the crime. At the same time, there is no need to forgive a repentant criminal, because in repenting of the crime, the criminal has already taken steps to erase it.[15]

Avengers, Forgive!

There is a potential conflict between forgiveness and a team called the "Avengers" that we need to address. To avenge and to forgive seem to be opposites. To avenge is to punish in order to right a wrong, while to forgive is to forgo punishment—or so it seems. In fact, avenging and forgiving can be united. Forgiving doesn't involve forgoing punishment—it involves forgoing resentment and revenge. Revenging and avenging are related, but distinct. Avenging has to do with justice, and may be sought by anyone, not just the victims of a crime or wrong-doing. Superheroes usually pursue justice in the names of the people they are sworn to protect, not for themselves. Revenge, on the other hand, is personal. I cannot revenge a wrong done to you—no offense, but I probably don't even know you. I can't feel the kind of personalized harm necessary for revenge.[16]

There is no conflict between avenging and forgiving because the Avengers (and avengers in general) can forgive as well as punish. For instance, there have been two occasions where an Avenger has been given the ultimate punishment—expulsion from the team—only to be readmitted later. Iron Man was expelled in the wake of the Armor Wars after he caused the death of the Gremlin,[17] and Hank Pym was expelled for a variety of bizarre actions, including attacking a foe who had already surrendered.[18] Both were welcomed back later; they were punished and then forgiven.

This is possible because punishment and forgiveness serve distinct purposes. Forgiveness is largely about reestablishing relationships, while punishment is usually about retribution. By violating the rules, these Avengers incurred debts to the rest of the team, and when they were punished they repaid those debts. Thus, Tony and Hank can be readmitted once they have paid for their crimes. Punishment as retribution can be thought of as making reparations for a crime—a step on the road to forgiveness. Still, while we may repay a debt by being punished, we should keep in mind that forgiveness can't be earned like a reward or a paycheck, which a person deserves, but must be granted voluntarily by the victim.

Ultimately, this is what we should take away from these reflections about the Avengers: We cannot demand forgiveness for past missteps, nor can forgiveness be demanded of us. We can, however, make it more (or less) reasonable to grant forgiveness through our subsequent behavior. Just asking for forgiveness may not merit it, but it certainly helps if the request shows the victim that the criminal acknowledges and owns the crime. Those Avengers, like Hawkeye, who are former criminals and villains, never deny what they did in their past lives, and their continuing service as heroes shows that they are worthy of forgiveness.

NOTES

1. Hannah Arendt, *The Human Condition* (Chicago: University of Chicago Press, 1998), 236–243.

2. *Avengers*, vol. 1, #9 (October 1964).

3. Bishop Joseph Butler, "Sermons VIII and IX," in *Fifteen Sermons* (London: Ware, Longman, and Johnson, 1774).

4. For a brilliant philosophical discussion of excuses, see J. L. Austin, "A Plea for Excuses," in *Philosophical Papers* (New York: Oxford, 1979), 175–204.

5. *Avengers*, vol. 1, #57 (October 1968), reprinted in *Essential Avengers Vol. 3* (2001).

6. *Avengers*, vol. 1, #54–55 (July–August 1968), reprinted in *Essential Avengers Vol. 3* (2001).

7. Claudia Card, *The Atrocity Paradigm: A Theory of Evil* (New York: Oxford University Press, 2002), chapter 8.

8. *X-Men*, vol. 1, #4 (March 1964), reprinted in *Essential Uncanny X-Men Vol. 1* (2010).

9. For more on this, see Charles Griswold, *Forgiveness: A Philosophical Exploration* (New York: Cambridge University Press, 2007).

10. For Tony's own issues with forgiveness and atonement, see Christopher Robichaud, "Can Iron Man Atone for Tony Stark's Wrongs?" in *Iron Man and Philosophy*, ed. Mark D. White (Hoboken, NJ: John Wiley & Sons, 2010), 53–63.

11. For that matter, could *anyone* forgive a mime?

12. What, no mime joke? Can't think outside the box? Ha-ha . . .

13. For instance, in *Avengers*, vol. 1, #401 (August 1996).

14. Jacques Derrida, *On Cosmopolitanism and Forgiveness*, trans. Mark Dooley and Michael Hughes (New York: Routledge, 2001), 32–33.

15. Leo Zaibert, "The Paradox of Forgiveness," *Journal of Moral Philosophy* 6 (2009): 365–393.

16. For more on the distinction between justice (or *retribution*) and revenge, see Robert Nozick, *Philosophical Explanations* (Cambridge, MA: Harvard University Press, 1981), 366–370.

17. *Iron Man*, vol. 1, #229 (April 1988), reprinted in *Iron Man: Armor Wars* (2007).

18. *Avengers*, vol. 1, #213 (November 1981).

GODS, BEASTS, AND POLITICAL ANIMALS: WHY THE AVENGERS ASSEMBLE

Tony Spanakos

The world needs what it always needs. Heroes.
Not S.H.I.E.L.D. Agents . . . Not H.A.M.M.E.R.
Agents. Avengers. Now, maybe more than ever.

—Steve Rogers[1]

When the *Avengers* title was relaunched in 2010, we were told that "Earth's Mightiest Heroes united against a common threat! On that day the Avengers were born—to fight the foes that no single hero could withstand!"[2] This was no surprise, since Stan Lee told true-believing fans essentially the same thing in the original *Avengers* #1 in 1963. But the claim is misleading, if not inaccurate. The Avengers may believe that they "assemble" in order to fight great foes, but there is more to it than this.

When not Avengers, they perform great world-saving deeds on their own, but they long for fellowship and they languish emotionally. (Even their solo superheroics are often done in tandem with fellow Avengers in the great tradition of the "Marvel team-up.") So what is the real reason why the Avengers assemble? Aristotle (384–322 BCE) would say that in working together as a community the Avengers act excellently (*arête*) and develop fellowship (*philia*).[3] Ultimately, through their common action, they flourish (*eudaimonia*). And that is why they assemble.

Assembling for Necessity or Perfection?

We can easily dismiss the claim that the Avengers came together out of necessity, to defeat a supervillain whom they could not defeat alone. The evidence for this is that the Avengers originally assemble to fight Loki, who confuses them into fighting the Hulk.[4] But even casual readers of Marvel Comics know that Thor fought Loki on his own throughout his long comics career. Loki is therefore not a foe whose defeat could only be secured by the concerted action of the Avengers. The same could be said of Kang, Modok, the Submariner, and many other Avenger villains who have also fought solo Avengers. Necessity hardly sustains the Avengers; there must be something else that makes them keep assembling.

Let's look at Aristotle's explanation of the creation of the city-state (*polis*) for suggestions. Man, not sufficient in himself to live in isolation, needs the *polis* to ensure reproduction, stability, security, and the possibility of exchange.[5] But while necessity might lead to forming a *polis*, it is maintained for reasons that go far beyond that. The *polis*, or city-state, is the political community that responded to something more fundamental in the lives of the Greeks. Put bluntly, "One cannot be a human being except in the context of a *polis*,"[6] and the man outside of the *polis* is either a god or beast.[7] A god does not need the *polis*, and a beast has neither use nor appreciation of it. For the mortal man in between, the *polis* is the place where fellowship (*philia*) is found, excellence (*arête*) is enacted, and human thriving (*eudaimonia*) is developed and perfected.

Aristotle's argument is based on his belief that man is a "political animal" (*zoon politikon*). But many of the Avengers are not ordinary humans. They are gods, mutants, and machines— one is even a Beast. It doesn't matter. One may join the Avengers for the same reason one joins Aristotle's *polis*, necessity. But one also remains in the Avengers for the same reason one remains in the *polis*, for the sake of the good life.

Elementary Greek Lessons (Approved by the Comics Code)

With all due respect to our good friend Ares, further elaboration on a few ancient Greek terms might help. The *polis* was different from other communities based on its size and the role of citizens in its social and political life.[8] Also, Aristotle's use of the word "political" is far broader than its use today. Having its roots in the life of the *polis*, politics for Aristotle encompasses the social, economic, and (what we call) political aspects of living in common with others. This distinction is important because, aside from a few examples such as Tony Stark's time as secretary of defense and head of S.H.I.E.L.D., most Avengers eschew "politics," even though they may be very political. Captain America, for example, is the living embodiment and symbol of the American spirit, but he refuses to run for president, only begrudgingly serving as head of U.S. security following Norman Osborn's "Dark Reign." In fact, he often avoids formal politics to engage in more meaningful and direct "political" action (saving the lives of citizens, defending the country from foreign/alien invasion, or simply being a role model to generations of Americans).

The Avengers do not form their own *polis* in the sense of an independent political unit (like Genosha or the various dwelling places of the Inhumans), but they do engage in political community. The reason that they do this—and the reason they keep returning to the Avengers—is that avenging allows them a path to attaining *eudaimonia* that is more perfect than they can achieve in their solo careers. Commonly translated as happiness or fulfillment, *eudaimonia* "consists . . . in satisfying the desires that are *necessary* for man to have in order to live a full, rich life."[9] But reading *eudaimonia* as "happiness" in the twenty-first-century sense may distort its meaning in a couple of ways: first, happiness might be read in a hedonistic way, and second, it might be seen as an internal condition. Aristotle would disavow both. The first can be discarded because a full life is one based on reason and not pleasure, and the second can be discarded because happiness is not a feeling but a way of being. Specifically, Aristotle's understanding of happiness (*eudaimonia*) involves virtue or excellence (*arête*), action that is practiced and developed over time. *Arête* is excellence in *doing* something, not simply an internal characteristic of the soul.[10] While it is often used in a moral sense, *arête* can also be used to characterize the excellence that a carpenter has in terms of building a house. In other words, it is excellence relative to the craft or function of the craftsman, and it reaches its acme in the field of ethics and political life because this is the function of *all* humans.[11]

X *Example of happy*

If *arête* is found in action within the community, it supplements and is supplemented by the development of fellowship or friendship, *philia* (last Greek word, I promise), between citizens. In the *Nicomachean Ethics*, Aristotle argues that "the happy man [*eudaimoni*] must have society. . . . And it is obviously preferable to associate with friends [*philon*] and with good men than with strangers and chance companions. Therefore the happy man requires friends."[12] *Philia* can develop for different reasons: advantage (I am friends with you because you can get me a job); pleasure (*Jersey Shore*'s Snooki enjoys hanging out with the

Sitch and JWoww because they are mad funny); or virtue (you are friends with me because you want what is good for me for my sake).[13] This last form of *philia*, "wanting for someone what one thinks good, for his own sake and not for one's own, and being inclined, so far as one can, to do such things for him," is the highest level of friendship.[14] In this version of friendship, the person sees his or her fellow as "another self" and finds in him or her someone also committed to *arête*: "Hence it is necessary for anyone who is going to be happy [*eudaimonisonti*] to have excellent friends [*philon*]."[15]

Superheroes, obviously, perform superheroic acts of excellence regularly, whether they are members of the Avengers or not. But even though they may stop crime and superpowered villains in their solo careers, their lives and acts are necessarily incomplete. Inevitably, the desire for *eudaimonia* leads them to return to the Avengers, or at least to regular interaction and team-ups.

 Anecdote

Ms.-sing Her Friends

> Jessica Jones: Remember the time you kept the . . . sun from exploding?!
>
> Ms. Marvel: You know what I did next? I went home and sat on my butt for six months, eating Ben & Jerry's and watching old movies.[16]

Following the "House of M" story arc, Carol Danvers "realized that she was not living up to her full potential as Ms. Marvel" and decided to emphasize her solo adventuring.[17] But, six months later, when she defeats Stilt-Man in battle, he does not recognize her, and her recently hired publicist gets her a spot on the TV show *Super Powers* called "Where Are They Now?"[18] She complains about this to Jessica Jones, another ex-Avenger, telling her that she left the Avengers because as an Avenger she waited for people to save, whereas, on her own, she goes out "on patrol" and "find[s] out you're needed before you're needed."[19] And yet when she sees some green aliens on the next two pages, her first instinct is to call Captain America. In fact, the entire first issue of her new comic book series is shaped not by her solo adventures, nor by forging her own identity, but by her inability to escape from being an Avenger.

Another important Avenger in Carol's life is Iron Man (Tony Stark), who is not just a fellow crimefighter but also a recovering alcoholic (like Carol) and Carol's sponsor for Alcoholics Anonymous.[20] So when he asks her to join and lead his Avengers team after the Marvel Universe "Civil War," this is coming from more than someone who *also* fights crime.[21] It is coming from a fellow on several levels, someone who understands her as few others can. After all, they not only act excellently together (in fighting crime), but they also find happiness in each other's excellence (staying sober, for instance).

In the first year of her solo run, Carol tries to find herself and realize her potential. Aristotle says the human function is to attain *eudaimonia*, and accordingly Ms. Marvel identifies her function, saying that "heroes need to . . . I need to make a difference."[22] Ironically, she only comes to this understanding once she decides to return to (and lead) the Avengers. Before she makes this decision, supervillains do not recognize her, TV producers consider her a has-been, and she has nothing resembling a "normal life."[23] Perhaps she cannot lead a normal life—not because she is a superhero, but specifically because she is an ex-Avenger.

Carol tries to explain herself to her publicist, who ultimately does not understand her and cannot form a bond of *philia* with her. By contrast, Jessica Jones really *gets* her on a personal level, and Carol also has deep, meaningful conversations with Captain America and Tony Stark. When she engages in the *arête* of a superhero, Carol usually does so with other former or actual Avengers (Doctor Strange, Tigra, Valkyrie).

Thus although she continues to act as a solo hero, she is not able to flourish the way she had hoped. When she finally understands what her purpose is, she fulfills it as an Avenger. On the cover of *Mighty Avengers* #1 and the opening splash page, Ms. Marvel glides down into battle, completely confident leading the Mighty Avengers, including veterans such as the Wasp, Wonder Man, the Black Widow, and Iron Man, all of whom are seasoned heroes. She finds *eudaimonia* among those with whom she shares *philia*, the Avengers.

Getting Her *Arête* Together

You were a mess . . . you weren't half the woman you've become over the last couple of years.

—Luke Cage to Jessica Jones[24]

Luke Cage (Power Man) uses these words, among others, to convince Jessica that he truly wants to marry her. She *was* a mess, and she *is* one of the most intriguing and compelling characters in Marveldom. She is perpetually unhappy, self-deprecating, and utterly lacking in self-confidence. Jessica gained her powers when she was exposed to some chemicals following a car accident that killed her parents and brother.[25] Prior to the accident, she was a miserable loner—so much so that she had a crush on Peter Parker and even *he* didn't notice her—but she is even more so following her accident, given her guilt over partially causing it. After her convalescence in the hospital, Jessica is given the good news that she can return to her old high school and that a foster family wants to adopt her.[26]

When Jessica returns she is more alienated than ever, treated like a freak by the cheerleaders, humiliated by the jocks, and pitied by Peter Parker.[27] In her frustration, she runs away and discovers she has superstrength and can fly, but she is still thoroughly unsatisfied. Describing her early superheroing, Jessica says she tried it "for about a week. And it wasn't a good week. It was an angry week. But I kept telling myself. There's people in need. People causing trouble. That was the excuse but really . . . I just wanted to hit things."[28] Years later, she gives up the "superhero game" and becomes a private detective.

Jessica seems to be perpetually looking for *eudaimonia*. More so than probably any Marvel character, she is a loner. Her fundamental repulsion at being a superhero makes it seem unlikely that she would need to be an Avenger. But like her friend Carol Danvers, she is miserable when she is *not* an Avenger. She drinks excessively, has meaningless trysts (repeatedly), uses foul language, and smokes like a chimney. There is no *eudaimonia*. She even yells at Carol when she urges Jessica to take on a case.[29] Despite her outburst, she knows that Carol is her friend. This is why Jessica, who trusts no one, can tell Carol about her one-night stand with Luke Cage (a former and future Avenger). Ironically, when Carol tells her that Luke is a "cape chaser" (dates only superheroines), she tries to set Jessica up with Scott Lang, a former Ant-Man.[30] In other words, although Carol criticizes Luke for only dating heroes, Jessica seems trapped in the same pattern—and not only "capes" but Avengers in particular.

In the series *The Pulse*, Jessica is already pregnant with Luke's child, and many of her fellow Avengers pitch in to help. Carol organizes a lunch with Jessica and Sue Richards (the Invisible Woman) because Jessica is worried about what her kid will be like, having two superheroes for parents.[31] Sue, also a former Avenger, allays Jessica's fears by telling her about the two kids she and Mr. Fantastic have. Later, Carol takes Jessica and Luke to the design studio of founding Avenger Janet van Dyne (the Wasp) to help Luke find a new superhero outfit.[32] When Jessica's water breaks, Carol flies her to the hospital, and when Luke can't get to the hospital because of heavy traffic, Jan issues the call, "Avengers Assemble!"[33] In their moment of human need, Jessica and Luke, both fiercely independent, get a little help from their friends—all of them Avengers.

Later, the woman in charge of the hospital insists on getting Jessica out of the hospital because "we cannot give birth to whatever she has in there! We don't know what kind of mutant is going to come out! She could give birth to an atomic bomb or—or a poison!!"[34] When she suggests sending Jessica to the Baxter Building or S.H.I.E.L.D., she is interrupted by Captain America, who says, "That won't be necessary. . . . We'll take her."[35] Cap, surrounded by the New Avengers, takes her to the house of Doctor Strange, a former Avenger, to give birth. During the birth, Ms. Marvel is right next to her, holding a cloth to her head.[36] While the paparazzi wait outside, powerless journalist Ben Urich wonders, "What about the person behind the mask . . . who needs help and friends and love just like the rest of us . . . Who will be there to help them when things don't go their way? When tragedy strikes?"[37] As if the point needed further clarification, Urich's narration is matched with images of Luke, Cap, Spidey, Spider-Woman, and Iron Man.

Together with Luke and a baby girl, Jessica becomes less dark; she's even happy at times. Interrupting her wedding to Luke, she inserts her own vows, telling him:

> I truly believe that together we are so much better than we are apart . . . I don't get lost in my own head like I used to. This world is a scary place. You being an Avenger—it's so . . . scary. Every day there's some idiot in our face trying to ruin it. And ever since we got together, I just haven't cared.[38]

This is an incredible statement from the (formerly) self-loathing Jessica Jones, the one who looks down on the superhero lifestyle. Being part of the Avenger community—best friends with the leader, marrying another, and a former Avenger herself—she finds *philia*. In her wedding photo, Jessica beams in the midst of the New Avengers, clearly among her own and, most important, having found her *eudaimonia*.[39] In fact, when Clint Barton (Hawkeye) is captured, and Luke is still recovering, Jessica joins Spider-Woman, Mockingbird, and Ms. Marvel to do battle as an Avenger again.[40]

The Original Irredeemable Ant-Man

I . . . stopped trying to figure out the Pyms a long time ago. I'm pretty sure they . . . drove me to drink in the first place.

—Tony Stark[41]

Over the last five decades, Henry (Hank) Pym has become one of Marvel's most flawed, and repulsive, heroes. When he first appeared in *Tales to Astonish*, volume 1, #27, in January 1962, he decided that his serums were "far too dangerous to ever be used by any human again!"[42] Nonetheless he returned eight issues later because "so great a discovery must not melt into nothingness!"[43] And indeed, Pym has been a character conflicted between doing the right thing and pursuing his science even when it consistently leads to disastrous results, such as physically abusing his wife, Janet van Dyne, or endangering the team in his poorly concocted efforts to get himself invited back into the Avengers after he was expelled.[44]

After one such screwup, Tigra calls him a "rat" and tells Jarvis that she is happy to see him gone. Ever the voice of wisdom, Jarvis cautions Tigra—and the reader—about being too judgmental. Although, in the words of Captain America, Pym is guilty of "misconduct before the enemy," Jarvis says, "He is a hero! Men are fallible—even heroes."[45] When Pym tries to apologize to Jan, she tells him, "I pity you. . . . You're a deeply troubled man! You need help!"[46] Eventually, he is reinstated, first as an adviser and then as a member of the West Coast Avengers.[47] In that capacity, he dates Tigra—yes, the same Tigra—contemplates suicide, and eventually gets back together with Jan (for the umpteenth time). Though she is beautiful, heroic, and an Avenger, Tigra is not Jan, the love of his life and the woman with whom he cofounded the Avengers. As with Carol and Jessica, Hank's *eudaimonia* is accomplished by being an Avenger and being *with* the Avengers, especially Jan.

Hank's latest reconciliation with the Avengers comes when Hercules and Amadeus Cho want to reconvene a new team of Avengers after Norman Osborn forms his own Avengers team (known to comics fans as the Dark Avengers).[48] They find Jarvis and he tells them, "There's only one man I can think of . . . to lead a team of new Avengers": Hank Pym.[49] Pym, at this point, is not Ant-Man, Giant Man, Goliath, or Yellowjacket, but the Wasp (an identity he takes in honor of his now deceased former wife). When Jarvis tells him, "There has come a day, sir, unlike any other, where earth's mightiest heroes must unite against a common threat," Pym interrupts him with, "Stop. The Avengers' oath, Jarvis. That won't work on me. Who do you think wrote it into the charter?"[50] Unfortunately, he is still Hank Pym, arrogant and self-centered. Previously he concocted all sorts of schemes (which backfired) to get back into the Avengers. Now, when they call him, he says, "I'm flattered. But I'm in the middle of something. And really? Me? There has to be someone else out there. Some other superhero."[51]

But as much as Hank is shirking his responsibility to save the world, he remains a sympathetic character. He tells the others that he is and has always been afraid of leading the Avengers. At first he felt that he could not "measure up" to Thor, Hulk, and Iron Man, until he came up with the plan that stopped Loki during their first adventure together. "That's when I realized what I brought to the table . . . I, Henry Pym, was the smartest man in the room. And whether the others realized it or not, I was their leader."[52] But he could not control the Giant Man serum, and one day he realized Tony Stark was Iron Man. "Next to him . . . I was less than nothing. And far from the smartest man in the room."[53]

Appropriately enough, in the next issue Iron Man humiliates Pym and tells him that he is taking over, to which Pym replies, "You can take over from here? You? Tony Stark? Mister fought-against-Cap-in-the-Civil-War. Shot-Hulk-into-space-and-caused-World-War-Hulk. Gave-the-Skrulls-everything-they-needed-to invade-Earth. You're taking over? Give me one good reason why." Stark responds, simply, "Three words . . . You're Hank Pym."[54] Pym stands down, but when he hears about some of Stark's recklessness while he was away (kidnapped by Skrulls), he begins to reconsider. When Pym takes on Chthon, the latter says, "It appears the only thing greater than how much the people of this world believe in me is how little they believe in you?" Pym says, "Well, y'know what? Screw all you! I don't care if any of you believe in me. I'm Hank Pym and I believe in myself. I'll fix this."[55]

Pym ultimately prevails in battle, helped by the Vision and the other Avengers. But the battle also shakes him from his arrogance and victimization. When Hercules says he owes him an apology, Pym says, "No, you did what you thought was right. I could ask no more of any Avenger. As for Iron Man . . . The Tony I knew was better than this. Something's up with him. He seemed . . . off his game." Despite having the opportunity to critique the man who humiliated him, Pym defends him, showing the sort of *arête* that we would not have thought possible of him, while also being a pillar of virtue for his fellow, Iron Man, as Aristotle would have hoped. When Pym flies after Tony, Tony says, "So. You're calling yourself the Wasp? And you're going to lead a new team? Those are big shoes to fill, Hank. Three words of advice. Don't screw up."[56] Not exactly heartwarming stuff, but Tony recognizes Pym's *arête* and accepts him as a fellow Avenger and a leader of a new Avengers group.

Neither Gods nor Beasts but Political Animals

"Superheroes . . . do not fit into the societies that they protect," which is why their personal lives are both important and incomplete.[57] In this chapter, we analyzed the way in which three Avengers' search for fulfillment (*eudaimonia*) involved their fellowship (*philia*) and practice of excellence (*arête*) within the community of the Avengers. Importantly, Ms. Marvel, Jessica Jones, and Hank Pym all languished in terms of morale, and at times morality, outside the Avengers. Finding their *eudaimonia* required the *philia* and the opportunities for *arête* made possible by lives intertwined with Avengerness, even if they periodically leave or get thrown out of the Avengers. It is noteworthy that the most self-loathing superhero, Jessica Jones, and the most repulsive superhero, Hank Pym, often return to the center of Avenger life and never leave its periphery. So, to update Aristotle, the Avengers have both gods and beasts, but even they are not self-sufficient; they need the *polis* in order to attain *eudaimonia*.[58]

NOTES

1. *Avengers*, vol. 4, #1 (July 2010), reprinted in *Avengers by Brian Michael Bendis Vol. 1* (2011).

2. Ibid.

3. Although *philia* is generally translated as "friendship," today that word suggests a voluntary relationship that Aristotle would not have understood. Also, *philia* is not purely friendship but also a sense of a common ethical and social identity, which is why Aristotle can speak of a form of civic *philia* among citizens in a *polis*.

4. *Avengers*, vol. 1, #1 (September 1963), reprinted in *Essential Avengers Vol. 1* (1998).

5. See Aristotle, *Politics*, 1252b29–1252b30 (any reputable translation will include this standard pagination), and also Christopher Shields, *Aristotle* (New York: Routledge, 2007), 352.

6. See C. C. W. Taylor, "Politics," in *The Cambridge Companion to Aristotle*, ed. Jonathan Barnes (Cambridge, UK: Cambridge University Press, 1995), 233–258, esp. at 239.

7. Aristotle, *Politics*, 1253, and *Nicomachean Ethics*, 1097b6–1097b16. When I quote from the *Nicomachean Ethics*, I use H. Rackham's translation available in *Aristotle: Nicomachean Ethics* (Cambridge, MA: Harvard University Press, 1934).

8. Taylor, "Politics," 235.

9. Jonathan Lear, *Aristotle: The Desire to Understand* (Cambridge: Cambridge University Press, 1998), 155.

10. Ibid., 153. The idea of virtue being something within the soul is associated with the influence of Christian ethics.

11. *Nicomachean Ethics*, 1097b16–1097b20.

12. Ibid., 1169b16–1169b22.

13. Ibid., 1168b11–1169a7.

14. John M. Cooper, "Aristotle on Friendship," in *Essays on Aristotle's Ethics*, ed. Amélie Oksenberg Rorty (Berkeley: University of California Press, 1980), 301–339.

15. *Nicomachean Ethics*, 1170b14–1170b19.

16. *Ms. Marvel*, vol. 2, #1 (May 2006), reprinted in *Ms. Marvel: Best of the Best* (2006).

17. *Ms. Marvel*, vol. 2, #13 (May 2007), reprinted in *Ms. Marvel: Operation Lightning Storm* (2007).

18. *Ms. Marvel*, vol. 2, #1.

19. Ibid.

20. *Ms. Marvel*, vol. 2, #13.

21. *Mighty Avengers* #1 (March 2007), reprinted in *Mighty Avengers: The Ultron Initiative* (2008).

22. *Ms. Marvel*, vol. 2, #13.

23. In terms of her love life, Carol had just one date, with a "normal" guy, which was (of course) interrupted by superheroing (*Ms. Marvel*, vol. 2, #11, March 2007, reprinted in *Ms. Marvel: Operation Lightning Storm*). Carol is more appropriately matched with Simon Williams (Wonder Man), whom she and Iron Man recruited for the Mighty Avengers, and who shows her true *philia* through his devotion to *arête* as a hero. (See their exchange in *Mighty Avengers: The Ultron Initiative*, 2008.)

24. *The Pulse* #14 (May 2006), reprinted in *The Pulse Vol. 3: Fear* (2006).

25. *Alias* #22 (July 2003), reprinted in *Alias Ultimate Collection Book 2* (2010).

26. Ibid.

27. *Alias* #23 (August 2003), reprinted in *Alias Ultimate Collection Book 2*.

28. *The Pulse* #14.

29. *Alias* #24 (September 2003), reprinted in *Alias Ultimate Collection Book 2*.

30. See *Alias Ultimate Collection Book 1* (2009).

31. *The Pulse* #11 (November 2005), reprinted in *The Pulse Vol. 3: Fear*.

32. Ibid.

33. *The Pulse* #12 (January 2006), reprinted in *The Pulse Vol. 3: Fear*.

34. Ibid.

35. Ibid.

36. Ibid.

37. Ibid.

38. *New Avengers Annual* #1 (June 2006), reprinted in *The Pulse Vol. 3: Fear*.

39. Ibid.

40. *New Avengers Annual* #3 (February 2010), reprinted in *New Avengers Vol. 13: Siege* (2010).

41. *Mighty Avengers* #1 (March 2007).

42. Reprinted in *Essential Ant-Man Vol. 1* (2002).

43. *Tales to Astonish*, vol. 1, #35 (September 1962), reprinted in *Essential Ant-Man Vol. 1*.

44. See *Avengers*, vol. 1, #212–214 (October–December 1981).

45. *Avengers*, vol. 1, #214 (December 1981).

46. Ibid.

47. *West Coast Avengers*, vol. 2, #21 (June 1987), reprinted in *Avengers: West Coast Avengers—Lost in Space and Time* (2012).

48. For more on the Dark Avenger, see the chapter titled "The Self-Corruption of Norman Osborn: A Cautionary Tale" by Robert Powell and the chapter titled "Shining the Light on the Dark Avengers" by Sarah Donovan and Nick Richardson in this volume.

49. *Mighty Avengers* #21 (March 2009), reprinted in *Mighty Avengers: Earth's Mightiest* (2009).

50. Ibid.

51. Ibid.

52. Ibid.

53. Ibid.

54. *Mighty Avengers* #22 (April 2009), reprinted in *Mighty Avengers: Earth's Mightiest*.

55. Ibid.

56. Ibid.

57. Vincent M. Gaine, "Genre and Super-Heroism: Batman in the New Millennium," in *The 21st Century Superhero: Essays on Gender, Genre, and Globalization in Film*, ed. Richard J. Gray II and Betty Kaklamanidou (Jefferson, NC: McFarland, 2011), 111–128, esp. at 127.

58. I am grateful to Mark White, Photini Spanakos, and William Batman Batkay for their comments.

CAP'S KOOKY QUARTET: IS REHABILITATION POSSIBLE?

Andrew Terjesen

In *Avengers*, volume 1, #16 (May 1965), the group went through its first major lineup change. All of the founding members of the Avengers quit, leaving only the "new kid," Captain America. The three new recruits were Hawkeye, who had fought Iron Man several times, and mutant twins Quicksilver and the Scarlet Witch, who were originally members of Magneto's Brotherhood of Evil Mutants. Quickly dubbed "Cap's Kooky Quartet," the Avengers became known for giving people second chances at leading heroic, virtuous lives. But is such rehabilitation possible?

Can an Archer Change His Trick Arrows?

Although his relationships with his fellow Avengers have been rocky due to his cocky nature and his need to prove himself (especially to Cap), Hawkeye is the most successful rehabilitation in Avengers history. He has been a part of the Avengers in some capacity for most of its existence, and he founded and led the West Coast Avengers. If we can pinpoint the source of Hawkeye's success, we could go a long way to understanding the nature of rehabilitation.

The word "rehabilitation" shares a Latin root with the word "habit." That Latin root means "to have, hold, or keep," which is fitting since rehabilitating someone involves breaking them of bad habits and making sure good habits take hold. The idea that a good person has a fixed and habitual character has a long history in moral philosophy and was best expressed by Aristotle (384–322 BCE) in the *Nicomachean Ethics*. According to Aristotle, a virtue is a fixed disposition that leads someone to choose the right way to act in a given situation. A virtuous person is not someone who is merely honest or courageous most of the time, or by accident or inclination. Rather, a virtuous person is *always* honest and courageous because that is who he or she *is*.

Being an honest person, however, does not mean always telling the truth or never being deceptive. Aristotle recognized that the right way to act was often dependent upon the circumstances of a specific situation, which is why a fixed character was needed. If honesty or courage could be summed up in terms of a rule, we would merely tell people to follow that rule. A virtuous person has the experience and fine-tuned moral sense to know what a situation demands. For example, no one would dispute that Captain America is courageous, but his courage is not defined by a particular set of rules. Sometimes his courage demands that he fight Thanos even if it seems likely that he is going to die, whereas other times courage demands that he make a strategic retreat or even surrender (as he did at the end of the Civil War).

If you're bothered by the idea that a virtuous person always does the virtuous thing, you're not alone. Contemporary philosopher and psychologist John M. Doris has challenged Aristotle's notion of character as being unrealistic, using psychological studies to show that it is impossible to develop the kind of fixed character that Aristotle seems to require.[1] These studies suggest that situational factors loom much larger than individual character in determining behavior. For example, in an infamous study conducted by psychologist Stanley Milgram, subjects were led to believe that they were part of an experiment testing the effects of negative reinforcement on learning. Subjects were told to give shocks to the learners if they got their answers wrong (though unbeknownst to the subjects, the learners were actually a part of the experiment and the shocks were faked). Milgram found that about two-thirds of all participants were willing to go "all the way" to 450 volts of shock (which would supposedly cause tremendous pain to the learner). Even people who reported leading virtuous lives outside this experiment went all the way.[2] Doris argues that the experiment created a situation where most people felt compelled to follow through with the shocks even if they thought it was the wrong thing to do. They weren't acting on virtues or vices, like courage or cruelty, but instead were reacting to the particular situation at hand.

Finding a Balance with Hawkeye

Doris argues that we don't really have global character traits like honesty, courage, or compassion that apply to a large number of situations regardless of their specific circumstances. Instead, we have local character traits, which apply more narrowly and in particular situations, like "courage under fire," or the "courage to speak out." So who is right, Aristotle or

Doris? The case of Hawkeye shows us that the answer may lie somewhere in between.

In Hawkeye's case, the relevant character trait seems to be a need for validation or attention. Just consider his reason for becoming a costumed adventurer: he was jealous of the attention Iron Man was getting.[3] This need for approval is a fixed part of Hawkeye's character; it is a constant theme in his solo stories as well as his adventures with the Avengers, the West Coast Avengers, and the Thunderbolts. Soon after donning his heroic mantle, though, Hawkeye was diverted into a criminal career. After he was mistaken for a criminal, his hotheadedness led him to decide spitefully that if they were going to think he was a criminal, he would become one.[4]

Hotheadedness and a need for approval are regional character traits, lying somewhere between the global traits described by Aristotle and the local traits defended by Doris. None of Hawkeye's regional character traits changed significantly when he went from criminal to hero. Although his experiences have tempered him somewhat, he remains the stereotypical costumed archer with a chip on his shoulder and a bad temper. Hawkeye's rehabilitation from a criminal to a hero did not eradicate those traits; instead, he used them for better purposes. His need for approval often leads him to try to prove his worth to his fellow heroes by taking the lead on risky missions, and because of his temper he is usually the Avenger who is most upset about perceived injustice and unfairness.

Avengers Annual #16 (1987) features one of Hawkeye's most memorable and notorious feats of heroism.[5] The Grandmaster has challenged the Avengers to stop his "lifebombs" from exploding and destroying the universe. The Avengers succeed, but the Grandmaster insists they replay that challenge, which they must do until the Grandmaster wins. At that point, Hawkeye challenges him to "draw straws" for the fate of the universe. In this case, the "straws" are Hawkeye's last two arrows, one of which has a trick attachment, and the one who

Ancedote

chooses this arrow is the winner. The Grandmaster can't resist this gamble and is shocked when he draws the shaft without an attachment, leaving him vulnerable just long enough to bring an end to his scheme. As we soon see, the Grandmaster actually chose the arrow with the attachment, but Hawkeye snapped the attachment off the arrow as the Grandmaster grabbed it. Cap criticizes Hawkeye for cheating, and later, at a baseball game, he tells Thor to watch Hawkeye closely because "he cheats!" Cap buys into the idea of cheating as a global character trait. As we know, though, Hawkeye is not someone who always cheats for his own gain. Rather, he has a regional character trait—say, being a rule bender for the sake of the greater good—that motivates his actions in a dire situation.

Maybe It Really Is in the Blood

The other members of the Kooky Quartet have not been as successful in staying on the side of the angels. Not many are fast enough to act more hastily than Hawkeye, but Quicksilver has no trouble outpacing our favorite archer's rash and hotheaded nature. He abruptly quits the Avengers after his sister Wanda is accidentally injured, and briefly joins up again with Magneto and even fights the X-Men.[6] Later he becomes an outright enemy of the West Coast Avengers. Throughout his career, Quicksilver ends up being as unpredictable as his name suggests. The Scarlet Witch is a more regular fixture on the Avengers roster until she becomes one of their greatest threats during the "Avengers Disassembled" story line, when she kills several Avengers, including her old friend Hawkeye and her former love the Vision.[7] After that, under her brother's influence, she uses her reality-altering powers to transform the world into the "House of M," where Magneto rules a mutant aristocracy that oppresses humans.[8]

Wanda and Pietro are the twin children of Magneto. Is there an unstable or evil gene that they inherited from their father? While that might be tempting to conclude, there is a simpler answer.[9] We already saw that Hawkeye's success depended on redirecting his existing character traits, but none of them were real obstacles to reform. If we look at Pietro and Wanda, we find that their experiences left them with some habits that were an impediment to becoming law-abiding members of the community.

As happens to many mutants in the Marvel Universe, Quicksilver and the Scarlet Witch were persecuted from an early age. This led them to join Magneto's Brotherhood of Evil Mutants, which seemed to be less concerned with fighting prejudice than with scheming for world domination. Because the Brotherhood only made things worse, the twins left and wrote a letter asking to join the Avengers. As Quicksilver explains, "The Avengers might accept us without caring that we are different—without always reminding us—we're mutants!!"[10] Wanda only reluctantly goes along with his plan; she would much rather that they stop using their powers and live in obscurity. Here we can see the differences between the two reflected in their regional character traits. Pietro is arrogant and takes the "scientific" name for mutants in the Marvel Universe—*Homo superior*—to heart. He wants to join the Avengers so that he can use his superspeed without being persecuted. Wanda, on the other hand, wants to live a normal life; she is more than happy to ignore her mutant nature.

Quicksilver's arrogance causes friction with Hawkeye and Cap, but he develops a grudging respect for them over time. It is not enough, however, to quell his distaste for humanity in general. At one point he tells his sister that it is humans, "with their constant mistrust of everything associated with the word mutant . . . who should try and please us!"[11] This is not the attitude of a hero, and it's no surprise that Quicksilver's sense of superiority is responsible for his backsliding into the role of villain. He feels that he deserves a certain level of respect, but the public at large remains fearful of him. After being wrongly blamed for an explosion, he says, "The time draws near when I will bear their insults and suspicions no longer . . . but will lash back!"[12] Aside from his arrogance, Pietro's defining characteristic is his love for his twin sister. When Wanda is injured in battle (which had secretly been caused by Magneto), Pietro's immediate response is to carry her off and quit the Avengers. When he finally returns to the Avengers, it's because his sister is in danger and he needs help.[13]

From that point forward, Pietro has a tumultuous association with the Avengers. Not only does he join and quit several times, but he also clashes with them as he tries to carry out villainous plots. Most of Wanda's tenure with the Avengers is a lot calmer, but she eventually uses her powers to destroy the Avengers as an organization and then reshape the world into a mutant paradise. Wanda's most defining characteristic is her simple desire to live a normal life—which she found with the Avengers—and unlike her brother she is more than willing to suppress her past experiences so that she can focus on the now.

When Aristotle talks about character, he distinguishes a virtuous person from a *continent* one. A virtuous person is someone who always does the right thing because it pleases them. For instance, a courageous person takes pleasure in doing the courageous thing. A continent person is someone who does the courageous thing but doesn't enjoy doing it. They probably do it because it is the "right thing to do," but they find doing the right thing to be burdensome. A virtuous person will not fall away from virtue, but a continent person could stumble under certain conditions. Both Quicksilver and Wanda seem to be continent as opposed to virtuous. Their experiences make it very hard for them to take true pleasure in behaving heroically. Hawkeye, by contrast, enjoys being a hero. It's not surprising then that the children of Magneto (especially Pietro) have a tendency to return to a life of villainy (what legal scholars call *recidivism*).

Old Dogs and New Tricks

When the Avengers were thought to be have been killed by Onslaught (and were really in the "Heroes Reborn" universe), the Masters of Evil pretended to be a group of superheroes known as the Thunderbolts.[14] Before long, however, some of the team realized they liked being superheroes and turned against their leader, Baron Zemo. When Hawkeye first read about the remaining Thunderbolts' claim that they had truly reformed, he was livid. In his usual hotheaded manner, he set out to confront them.[15] Why was he so skeptical about the Thunderbolts' rehabilitation when he had been in a similar situation upon joining the Avengers?

To begin with, he had not been a criminal long before reforming, whereas the Thunderbolts were mostly longtime villains before pretending (and later deciding) to be heroes. Akin to the distinction between virtue and continence is that between vice and incontinence. Vice is due to a negative trait, like cruelty, and incontinence is more like a lack of self-control with regard to exercising good traits (like kindness) when temptation to do otherwise strikes. A cruel person hurts people and takes pleasure in it, while an impulsive person may hurt people but feel remorse or regret about it. Since he or she is not truly vicious, the incontinent person is someone whose disposition is still open to change. The incontinent person could learn to overcome bad habits and embrace good ones. For example, Hawkeye never took pleasure in his criminal actions and felt bad about what he was doing when he was working with the Black Widow. So he was primed for rehabilitation.

The longer someone engages in a life of crime, though, the more likely it is that they will become twisted into a vicious person. We can see this if we look at the original Thunderbolts. Moonstone had spent her entire life learning how to manipulate people to get what she wanted. So when Hawkeye offers to lead the Thunderbolts so that they can earn their chance at redemption, she supports it because she thinks she can manipulate Hawkeye. She even tries to seduce him, though it seems that she actually ends up developing feelings for him—feelings that appear to go against her tendency to manipulate, suggesting the possibility that she will be truly reformed. However, their relationship falls apart and she embraces her old ways. Her manipulative nature is just who she is, an element of her viciousness.

In contrast to this, several other Thunderbolts were driven to the Masters of Evil originally by circumstances that would probably have made anyone engage in antisocial behavior. Songbird (who started her career as the villain Screaming Mimi) was abused by her father and later her partner in crime. Her resulting villainous behavior was simply a way to protect herself. As she began to feel more secure, she found it easier to embrace the heroic lifestyle, and eventually she became the warden of the Raft, a prison for supervillains, under the command of Luke Cage.[16] Part of her sense of security came from the relationship she formed with Abner Jenkins, originally the Beetle and then MACH-1, a mechanic who built his own super suit to commit crimes. By his own admission, he was really just looking for some respect, which he found with the Thunderbolts. He was then able to put his villainous persona behind him and become a hero. Unlike Moonstone, Songbird and the Beetle do not have negative character traits that are too solidified to reform, so they can successfully be rehabilitated and serve the world as heroes.

Avenging or Saving?

When Hawkeye took over the Thunderbolts, he lied to them, saying that the Commission on Superhuman Activities had agreed to pardon them if they started operating as heroes. Actually, when Hawkeye approached the commission about amnesty, he was told that it was impossible because they were longtime criminals and deadly threats. One commission member summed up the objection with a simple question: "If they act nice from now on, they don't have to pay for their crimes?"[17] This is the heart of most people's objection to rehabilitation as an alternative to punishment: it seems like an inappropriate, if not blatantly wrong, response to criminal behavior.

Most philosophical justifications of punishment fall into one of two general types: deterrence and retributivism. *Deterrence* focuses on preventing crime, punishing criminals both to prevent those criminals from committing new crimes (specific deterrence) and also to provide incentives for other people not to commit them (general deterrence). An advocate of deterrence would worry that rehabilitation programs could lead to higher crime rates if they are seen as "softer" or providing a way out of traditional punishment. On the other hand, proponents of *retributivism* maintain that criminals deserve punishment as a matter of justice, not because of any beneficial consequences from it. Before taking over the Thunderbolts, Hawkeye demands that any murderers on the team be prosecuted, saying murder is "one crime that I can't overlook. That can't be glossed over no matter how heroic you are afterward."[18] Retributivists give different reasons why crimes deserve punishment: some argue that punishment restores the balance of right and wrong after a crime is committed, while others stress the importance of expressing condemnation or disapproval of the wrongdoing.[19]

The reluctance to forgo punishing a hardened criminal is understandable, but our intuitions often change when it comes to young offenders. In these cases, it is difficult to balance the desire to give young people a chance to redeem themselves with the fear of suggesting to them that their crimes are not serious wrongs against society. After bringing an end to Norman Osborn's "Dark Reign," the Avengers had to decide what to do with the children that Osborn had detained and tortured in order to jump-start their superpowers. The Avengers feared that the kids' experiences being tortured by Osborn, coupled with the deadly side effects of their powers, would make them much more likely to become supervillains in the future.

To prevent this, Hank Pym had the idea that the teenagers should be enrolled in an Avengers Academy and trained to be heroes. Before long, though, the students crack Pym's files and discover that the Academy isn't about training those with the greatest potential for heroism, but instead about trying to intervene with those who have greatest potential for villainy.[20] The Academy is put to the test when several of the students sneak off to torment the Hood, a villain who had led an assault against their teacher Tigra.[21] When Tigra discovers what the kids did, her immediate response is to expel everyone involved. Pym thinks this is too harsh, though, and convenes a meeting to discuss their punishment. Another Academy teacher, Speedball, who was involved in the Stamford incident that killed six hundred people (and led to the Civil War), argues against expulsion because "these kids haven't done anything that they can't come back from."[22] The students are put on probation and told that the next mistake they make will get them kicked out of the Academy. They may have had tragic lives before coming to the Academy, but these kids are not hardened criminals. Rehabilitation seems (even more) justified in their case because they have their entire lives to try to be good, virtuous people.

Hope for the Future?

Kang, one of the Avengers' greatest enemies, seems an odd candidate for rehabilitation, but let's give our favorite time-hopping tyrant a chance. At one point, Kang traveled back in time to spare his younger self a savage beating by bullies, and then proceeded to show young Kang all the "great" things he would accomplish later in life. Older Kang didn't count on his younger self being appalled by what he would become, however. Instead of accepting his future, the young Kang stole his older self's time-travel technology and went even farther into the past. Masquerading as Iron Lad, he formed the Young Avengers to fight Kang.[23] To protect his friends, Iron Lad killed Kang—which is to say, he killed himself, albeit a different version of himself. By killing himself, Kang creates a new reality in which the Avengers died early in their careers and many of the Young Avengers were never born. Iron Lad then comes to realize that he has to go back to his own time and become Kang in order to undo his own death at his own hand.[24]

The story of Iron Lad illustrates several themes of this chapter. The only way that an unrepentant villain like Kang could become a hero would be if he were caught at a young age before his villainous nature had solidified. In fact, it is revealed that the severe beating that Kang rescued his younger self from was the catalyst for his transformation into a villain. Without that experience, his intellect and sense of adventure led him in a different direction. We also have evidence of Iron Lad's good character because he makes the ultimate sacrifice for the common good: he gives up his existence as a hero in order to save his friends. As even more evidence indicating a fundamental change in Kang's character, Iron Lad's brain patterns become the model for the revived Vision, who has since rejoined the Avengers as a trusted hero.

The Young Avengers—at least a generation away from Cap's Kooky Quartet—also give us a great example of when rehabilitation should trump punishment. Patriot is the grandson of Isaiah Bradley, the "Black Captain America" from *Captain America: Truth* (2009). He wants to be a hero like his grandfather, but he did not inherit his grandfather's supersoldier physiology. So in order to join the Young Avengers, Patriot claims that he got his grandfather's powers after a blood transfusion. To maintain this ruse, he began using the drug MGH (Mutant Growth Hormone) to give himself enhanced strength and durability. Since the drug is illegal, he obtains his supply by busting MGH dealers and seizing some of their product.[25]

When an attempt to get some MGH from a supervillain's lab goes awry, Patriot's lies are exposed. Although he has committed a crime by possessing MGH, no one demands he be punished, presumably because his intentions were good and he had not been engaging in this behavior for very long. Most important, he recognizes that he should give up being a Young Avenger because he lied to his teammates. Patriot's regional character traits (his desire to help people, loyalty to his teammates, and ability to inspire them) are the seeds of a real hero. The rest of the Young Avengers recognize this and invite him to rejoin the team, reaffirming the value of rehabilitation over punishment in his case.

Avengers Rehabilitate!

Rehabilitation can be a justifiable alternative under certain conditions. It works best if it is done early in someone's character development, before they develop truly vicious character traits. Rehabilitation can be appropriate if it is in response to crimes that are not deemed inexcusable. And finally, there needs to be a clear indication that the person to be rehabilitated is already trying to resist the negative effects of their regional character traits. Patriot's willingness to give up his spot on the Young Avengers suggests the kind of remorse that deserves a second chance, but Hawkeye always seemed to be an odd case. To try to impress the Avengers he broke into their mansion, tied up Jarvis, and then freed him with an impossibly difficult trick shot—which hardly seems to be a sincere and effective way to announce that you've given up a life of crime in hopes of becoming one of Earth's Mightiest Heroes![26] To merit rehabilitation, it is important that our former criminal display the underlying heroic traits, such as concern for others and lack of interest in being rewarded for one's heroic actions. Out of the three "problematic" members of Cap's Kooky Quartet, only Hawkeye shows clear evidence of rehabilitation, because only he has the right kind of regional traits that show promise of future heroism.

NOTES

1. Doris's arguments are summarized in his book *Lack of Character: Personality and Moral Behavior* (Cambridge: Cambridge University Press, 2002).

2. The full setup of Milgram's experiment and an analysis of the results can be found in his book *Obedience to Authority: An Experimental View* (New York: Harper and Row, 1974).

3. *Tales of Suspense* #57 (September 1964), reprinted in *Essential Iron Man Vol. 1* (2002).

4. For more on Hawkeye's self-doubt and need for validation, see the chapter by Mark D. White titled "The Way of the Arrow: Hawkeye Meets the Taoist Masters" in this volume.

5. Reprinted in *Avengers: The Contest* (2010).

6. They quit in *Avengers*, vol. 1, #49 (February 1968), reprinted in *Essential Avengers Vol. 3* (2001).

7. *Avengers Disassembled* (2005). On the relationship between the Scarlet Witch and the Vision, see the chapter by Charles Klayman titled "Love Avengers Style: Can an Android Love a Woman?" in this volume.

8. *House of M* (2006).

9. For more on the effects of Pietro and Wanda's parentage, see the chapter by Jason Southworth and Ruth Tallman titled "The Avengers: Earth's Mightiest Family" in this volume.

10. *Avengers*, vol. 1, #16 (May 1965), reprinted in *Essential Avengers Vol. 1* (1998).

11. *Avengers*, vol. 1, #45 (October 1967), reprinted in *Essential Avengers Vol. 2* (2000).

12. *Avengers*, vol. 1, #46 (November 1967), reprinted in *Essential Avengers Vol. 2*.

13. *Avengers*, vol. 1, #75 (April 1970), reprinted in *Essential Avengers Vol. 4* (2005).

14. *Thunderbolts* #1 (April 1997), reprinted in *Thunderbolts Classic Vol. 1* (2011).

15. *Avengers*, vol. 3, #8 (September 1998), reprinted in *Avengers Assemble Vol. 1* (2004).

16. *Thunderbolts* #144 (July 2010), reprinted in *Thunderbolts: Cage* (2011).

17. *Thunderbolts* #21 (December 1998).

18. Ibid.

19. For more on the philosophy of punishment, see Antony Duff, "Legal Punishment," *Stanford Encyclopedia of Philosophy*, http://plato.stanford.edu/entries/legal-punishment.

20. As revealed in *Avengers Academy* #1 (August 2010), reprinted in *Avengers Academy: Permanent Record* (2011).

21. *Avengers Academy* #8 (March 2011), reprinted in *Avengers Academy: Will We Use This in the Real World?* (2011).

22. *Avengers Academy* #9 (April 2011), reprinted in *Avengers Academy: Will We Use This in the Real World?*

23. *Young Avengers: Sidekicks* (2006).

24. For more on the paradoxes of time travel (and Kang), see the chapter by Andrew Zimmerman Jones titled "Can Kang Kill His Past Self? The Paradox of Time Travel" in this volume.

25. *Young Avengers: Family Matters* (2007); the entire run of *Young Avengers* has since been reprinted in a single hardcover collection, *Young Avengers* (2008).

26. The oddity of Hawkeye's application for Avengers membership was retconned recently (*Hawkeye: Blindspot*, 2011). Jarvis let Hawkeye into the mansion and was a willing participant in this strange job application because Hawkeye had risked his life to save Jarvis's mother from muggers. This retcon shows how important it is that the offer of rehabilitation go to someone who has evidenced the right kind of regional traits.

PART FOUR

DO THE AVENGERS EVER
GO TOO FAR?

FIGHTING THE GOOD FIGHT: MILITARY ETHICS AND THE KREE-SKRULL WAR

Christopher Robichaud

One of the most famous episodes in the ongoing exploits of the Avengers is their involvement in the Kree-Skrull War, an intergalactic conflict between two advanced alien civilizations that spanned galaxies and lasted millennia.[1] When the mighty Avengers confront Ronan the Accuser, the Supreme Intelligence, the Skrull shape-shifters, and the Kree Sentry 459, they appear outmatched and out of their league. When they uncover a plan by Ronan, a Kree, to reverse the evolution of humans, or when they encounter a plot by the government (strongly influenced by the Skrulls) to impugn the Avengers with conspiracy charges, they seem ill-prepared to overcome the vast forces aligning against them and the rest of us.

Of course, at the end of the day the Avengers prevail, with the help of their friend Rick Jones's love of 1940s superhero characters. While it may seem obvious that the Avengers were justified in their involvement, some challenging questions arise when we step back to take a hard look at the Kree-Skrull conflict in terms of military ethics.

Entry Point to the Kree-Skrull War

The Avengers weren't aware of the Kree-Skrull War until they were unwittingly thrust into it by a run-in with Captain Marvel, who was once a renowned Kree soldier called Mar-Vell. Mar-Vell was sent to Earth at the start of our space age as a spy for the Kree. His goal was to observe the emergence of superheroes and the explosion of our technological advances, which concerned the Kree. But Mar-Vell had a change of heart after arriving here and refused to follow his orders, instead becoming Captain Marvel, defender of Earth (and becoming seen, inaccurately, as a traitor to the Kree).

At the start of the Kree-Skrull story line in *Avengers*, a true Kree traitor, Ronan the Accuser, has succeeded in temporarily overthrowing the reign of the Kree leader, the organic computer known as the Supreme Intelligence. Part of his effort was motivated simply by a thirst for power, but he also thought that the Kree ought to be governed by themselves, not a machine.[2] Recognizing the strategic importance of Earth, and embracing the worry that humans are advancing too quickly, Ronan decides to make the conquest of Earth a central part of his strategy of maintaining Kree dominance. The opportunity to take down Captain Marvel along the way is an added bonus for him.

So at the very beginning of the Avengers' involvement in the Kree-Skrull War, they find themselves dealing with one Kree who wants to protect Earth and another who wants to conquer it—and the Skrulls haven't even entered the picture yet! If things seem a bit complicated already, don't worry. The story line of the Kree-Skrull War is notorious for making even the most die-hard fans scratch their heads. But whatever their narrative flaws, from the standpoint of military ethics these complications lend an important degree of authenticity to a fantasy war story. When it comes to actual military conflicts, nothing is ever simple and rarely is anything straightforward, especially in terms of ethics.

Nations often go to war using moral language that is black and white. We're the good guys fighting the bad guys; our soldiers are the heroes and theirs are the villains; and on and on. This tends to make everything seem simple, straightforward, and tidy; the story of the Kree-Skrull War, however, is anything but. Seeing that war, even as portrayed in a superhero comic book, is complicated can make us appreciate the moral complexity of war in the real world. If nothing else, we learn that our moral assessments of governments, individuals, and specific actions in wartime need to be more nuanced, careful— and, yes, more complicated—than we might initially expect.

There's an Intergalactic War Going On and You're Invited

Ronan the Accuser is leading the Kree in a war against the Skrulls, and his plan includes "devolving" humans so Earth can be used as a base in his efforts. If successful, this will kill two birds with one stone: it will eliminate the threat that humans will supposedly pose to the Kree one day, and it will provide a strategic location to use against the Skrulls. With that said, the Avengers find themselves smack dab in the middle of a cosmic conflict. Which side, if any, should they join? To answer that question, the Avengers must first determine whether either side is morally justified in fighting the war, which is often not as easy to determine as we might hope. But in the case of the Kree-Skrull War, the Avengers don't need to decide who's justified right away, because their primary role in the conflict is clear: protect Earth. In *just war theory*, this is the strongest justification for entering a conflict: self-defense.

One of the most important topics discussed in just war theory is determining the conditions that justify one nation in waging war upon another. Contemporary philosopher Michael Walzer argues that a morally permissible war must have a just *cause*.[3] Scholars disagree on what exactly this means, but for our purposes "cause" can be understood as what someone cares about or fights for: it's the *reason* for waging a war.[4] And for Walzer, among others, the strongest moral reason a nation can have for going to war is to defend itself against an act of aggression.

An act of aggression violates a nation's political sovereignty and often its territorial integrity as well. Nations have a right to both these things, which according to Walzer stem from the rights of individual citizens. An act of aggression by one nation against another, then, is a violation of the rights of citizens, who in turn have a right to defend themselves against such violations. More important, though, we don't have an absolute right to self-defense. For instance, we aren't allowed to defend ourselves against a military incursion into Alaska by completely annihilating Russia; the response wouldn't be proportional to the attack. We also aren't allowed to use military force if we haven't exhausted all other options, including diplomacy. Some just war theorists go so far as to argue that we aren't allowed to defend ourselves militarily if we have good reason to believe that war won't stop the aggression, because more harm will be caused without much good coming from it.

In considering the Avengers' initial involvement in the Kree-Skrull War, we're going to have to make some adjustments. Most obviously, nations aren't involved so much as entire peoples: the Kree, the Skrulls, and humanity. Walzer's account is based on the idea of a nation performing an aggressive act that violates another nation's right to political sovereignty or territorial integrity. The problem is that Earth as a whole has no such rights, since it isn't a political entity. All the same, we can consider an unjustified attack against humanity as simultaneous acts of aggression against each nation of Earth by the Kree "nation," led by Ronan. Admittedly, Ronan's efforts to devolve the human race start on a remote base in the Arctic Circle, but his "Plan Atavus" is intended to be leveled against the entire human race.

When the Avengers arrive on the scene, the plan has begun. An attack is under way against the human race, and thus a defensive war—starting with a counterattack by the Avengers—is morally justified, as long as the other conditions hold. Does taking out Ronan meet the proportionality requirement? It seems to; after all, they don't aim to destroy the entire Kree Empire. Is an Avengers strike the last resort? Admittedly, not much time is spent trying to reason with Ronan; but then, as with so many comic book villains, he doesn't present himself as open to rational discussion. Will the Avengers' strike reduce the overall harm from the conflict? They face quite a fight, but the stakes for humanity are extremely high and they have no compelling reason to believe they will fail.[5]

Was Ronan in the Right?

We've been assuming that Ronan's effort to devolve us is indeed an act of aggression, an unjustified act of war against the people of Earth, which itself justifies a defensive response on the part of the Avengers. But that's not how the Kree see it, of course: Ronan hopes to prevent us from becoming a threat to the Kree down the road.

Let's suppose, for the sake of argument, that this is the only reason Ronan is initiating his Plan Atavus. Is he morally justified in starting a preventive war? A preventive war is a war fought against a nation that isn't an immediate threat but is considered likely to become one down the road. Some just war theorists think that such wars are morally justifiable on consequentialist grounds, because fewer lives will be lost if a war of aggression can be stopped before it starts.

One obvious problem with preventive wars is that it is often difficult to determine what a nation's intentions are. Without strong and compelling evidence on that count, it seems that initiating a preventive war would be wholly unjustifiable. Wars would be waged all the time on nothing but informed hunches (or claims of such) that one country might have it in for another country at some time in the future. We'd be in a never-ending state of war, hardly a world anyone would want to live in. That is not to say that there could never be a scenario in which rock-solid evidence came to light regarding a nation's nefarious long-term plans. But we have to imagine that those situations will be extremely rare.

When it comes to the Kree, it's clear that they don't have enough evidence to conclude that we intend to be a threat to them down the road, if and when we ever develop the necessary technology to be a threat. Until the Avengers arrived on the scene, the people of Earth weren't aware the Kree even existed! Furthermore, it seems that the Kree's fears were influenced by their own history, not ours. Eons ago, the Skrulls traveled to other planets looking for trading partners. When they came to the planet Hala, they encountered two races, the Cotati and the Kree, who competed to determine which the Skrulls would trade with. The Cotati won, but the Kree turned on them and the Skrulls, stealing the latter's technology, which they used to develop technology of their own to launch an offensive against the Skrulls. Hence the Kree-Skrull War began.

Based on their own behavior, the Kree must suspect that once our planet develops sufficient technology, we will act just as belligerently toward the other races we encounter in our exploration of the galaxy. Given that humans have demonstrated little ability or inclination to live in peace with each other, this isn't entirely unreasonable. All the same, such speculation is still not enough to launch an annihilating strike against an entire species as the Kree under Ronan try to do. Even preventive wars are supposed to be a last-ditch action when diplomacy has failed, not an opening salvo.

Those Sneaky Skrulls

So much for the Kree's role in all of this—what about the Skrulls? Were they simply the victims of the aggressive Kree? In the beginning perhaps they were, but by the time the Avengers enter the fray, the Skrulls have been fighting the Kree for thousands of years. Furthermore, being shape-shifters, they have also infiltrated Earth, posing at various times as superheroes, government agents, and even cows.[6] Like the Kree, they recognize Earth's strategic potential in their ongoing conflict. Unlike the Kree—in particular, unlike Ronan—they did not launch a direct attack against us. Instead, their immediate goal in the story we're focusing on is to capture Mar-Vell and force him to make a device, the Omni-Wave Projector, that they can use as a weapon against the Kree.

Let's suppose that the Skrulls are fighting a just war against the Kree at this point, defending themselves against an aggressive enemy that has built an empire upon violence and stolen technology. Mar-Vell is no longer a soldier of the Kree, but neither is he willing to put a weapon of mass destruction into the hands of the Skrulls to use against his people. It is very unlikely that we could justify the Skrulls' using such a weapon against the Kree, even though the war between them has already lasted for centuries upon centuries and had cost countless lives. All the same, assuming that merely possessing the weapon and threatening to use it would bring the war to a close, what means can the Skrulls legitimately use to get Captain Marvel to put this weapon into their hands? In terms of military ethics, this is not a question about when it is morally permissible to *start* a war but rather about what it is morally permissible to *do* during a war.

The Skrulls' first strategy is to trick Captain Marvel, using their shape-shifting abilities to pretend to be Carol Danvers (an ally of Mar-Vell and the future Ms. Marvel) and convince him to build the Omni-Wave Projector. He does build it, but soon catches on to their ruse and immediately destroys it, which is good news for the Kree. Still, was the Skrulls' deception itself permissible? Most of us don't maintain a strict prohibition against lying or other forms of deception, especially if lives are at stake. Supposing the device, when in the hands of the Skrulls, could bring about the war's end (whether it had to be used or not), then the deception may be justified because it resulted in a smaller cost in terms of lives lost.[7]

Tortured Logic

But the next tactic—on the part of the Skrulls this time—is more questionable. The emperor of the Skrulls threatens to kill the captured Scarlet Witch and Quicksilver if Captain Marvel doesn't build *them* the device. He doesn't consider this a violation of the "Convention of Fornax," which is no doubt akin to our Geneva Convention and which prohibits combatants in the Kree-Skrull War from being tortured by the enemy. Is the emperor correct in his assessment, though? Is threatening Captain Marvel with the execution of his friends and allies—indeed, forcing him to witness their demise unless he makes the Projector—a kind of torture?

Plausibly, yes—and that's even if the emperor is bluffing. An action designed to make prisoners of war suffer significant mental duress so that they will provide information falls under the category of torture. Examples include regularly causing people sexual humiliation, forcing them to witness the desecration of objects they hold sacred, depriving them of sleep, or making them listen to their fellow prisoners suffer physical violence. In the case of Captain Marvel, threatening him with having to witness his friends' deaths unless he does something is torture. So are the Skrulls morally permitted to do this?

The very fact that the action counts as torture might be enough to determine the answer. To many people, it makes no sense to ask whether torture is wrong. But most military ethicists leave it an open question as to whether all acts of torture are impermissible, and even people who assert that torture is always wrong have different opinions as to why it's wrong. For some, it all boils down to consequences. On this view, torture—whether practiced or merely threatened—leads to more bad consequences than good ones. Rather than useful information, the thinking goes, bad information is obtained, leading to ineffective actions, and perhaps retaliatory abuse. This view aligns itself nicely with the moral theory called *consequentialism*, which maintains that actions are right or wrong depending solely on the outcomes of those actions: specifically, whether those actions maximize the overall good.

On a different view, torture is impermissible even if the consequences are good—even if valuable information is gleaned that leads to effective action and our soldiers aren't endangered because of it. According to this view, torture fails to treat enemy soldiers and combatants with the moral respect that all persons are owed. Following the philosopher Immanuel Kant (1724–1804), supporters of this position see torture as treating persons merely as means and not at the same time as ends in themselves.[8] Causing someone significant mental duress just to get them to provide useful information is tantamount to using this person instead of respecting him or her as a whole person. This way of thinking about torture falls broadly into *deontology*, which holds that there is more to the morality of actions than their consequences alone; instead, there is moral status inherent in an act itself, regardless of its outcome.[9]

We will leave it open as to which of these arguments better explains the common intuition regarding torture; it is enough to acknowledge that several lines of reasoning are available to support opposition to it. And if we accept that torture is wrong, we can conclude that even if the Skrulls are fighting a just war against the Kree, and even if the Projector would bring it to a close without costing lives, it is still wrong for them to torture Captain Marvel in pursuit of their goal. If we relax some of these questionable assumptions, we can say further that whatever circumstances led the Skrulls to being dragged into this war, they are no longer innocent participants in it.

And the War Rages On

Who wins the Kree-Skrull War? Neither side, really. In the particular story we've been focusing on, a beaten—but by no means defeated—Supreme Intelligence comes into the mix at the last minute and empowers the honorary Avenger Rick Jones to put an end to that round of fighting. But as those familiar with these two alien races know, this is hardly the end of the matter. More recently, the Skrulls invaded Earth yet again in *Secret Invasion* (2008–2009), which painted a much darker picture of their involvement in Earth's affairs. For now, though, we must rest content with having used the Kree-Skrull War as an opportunity to examine some of the issues that occupy the work of military ethicists, issues quite relevant to all of us, and about which careful reflection is still much needed.[10]

NOTES

1. The story that will be discussed in this chapter is collected in the volume *Avengers: Kree-Skrull War* (2008), which reprints *Avengers*, vol. 1, #89–97 (June 1971–March 1972), also reprinted (in black and white) in *Essential Avengers Vol. 4* (2005).

2. For more on organic machines and their status compared to humans, see the chapter by Charles Klayman titled "Love Avengers Style: Can an Android Love a Human?" in this volume.

3. See his *Just and Unjust Wars: A Moral Argument with Historical Illustrations*, 4th ed. (New York: Basic Books, 2006). For more on Walzer and just war theory, see the chapter

by Louis P. Melançon titled "Secrets and Lies: Compromising the Avengers' Values for the Good of the World" in this volume.

4. Walzer's book covers matters in much greater detail than we will be able to here. For a brief yet thorough introduction to the morality of war, see Brian Orend, "War," *Stanford Encyclopedia of Philosophy*, http://plato.stanford.edu/entries/war.

5. Also, many just war theorists believe that a war can't be just unless its declaration has political authority. The closest thing to an international body that could give the Avengers' actions political legitimacy in this sense would be the United Nations, and they're not in the picture at the time of the Kree-Skrull War. For more on the Avengers and governments, see the chapter by Arno Bogaerts titled "The Avengers and S.H.I.E.L.D.: The Problem with Proactive Superheroics" in this volume.

6. Yes, cows, albeit not by choice, but as a result of their battle with the Fantastic Four.

7. For more on the ethics of secrecy and deception, see the chapter by Melançon (cited in note 3) in this volume.

8. See Kant's *Groundwork of the Metaphysics of Morals*, Section II.

9. For more on consequentialism and deontology, see the chapter by Mark D. White titled "Superhuman Ethics Class with the Avengers Prime" in this volume.

10. Many thanks to the devoted, anonymous fans out there who, in articles on Wikipedia and forums, helped me fill in the blanks on some of the more recondite angles to the characters who appear in "The Kree-Skrull War."

SECRETS AND LIES: COMPROMISING THE AVENGERS' VALUES FOR THE GOOD OF THE WORLD

Louis P. Melançon

> The Avengers don't belong to any one country or government. We are and we always have been Earth's mightiest heroes. We're here for every man, woman and child on this planet. And I promise we're going to do right by you.
>
> —Hank Pym[1]

Superheroes have duties and must live by rules. For example, if there's a mother and baby crossing the street, don't let a rampaging monster throw a mid-1970s sedan at them. (Or at least make sure they don't get hit by it.) Often these rules are formalized when superheroes form teams, and most all the incarnations of the Avengers fit this bill. The founding members of the original Avengers team even took the time to codify their duties in a set of rules, a charter that most of the later teams, except the Dark Avengers, adhere to. (And since the Dark Avengers were chock full of murderers and psychopaths, they don't really count. Sorry, Norman.)[2] Their charter is one of the things that defines what the Avengers are, as well as what it means to be an Avenger as an individual: abiding by a set of rules or standards. But whether in the real world or the Marvel Universe, it can be difficult or even impossible to adhere to all of them, all of the time.

In particular, there is a tension between the need to keep the rules and the need to achieve certain results. Sometimes compromises must be made. We're not talking about things that happen in the heat of battle, or unintended consequences of what is otherwise a rule-abiding action. We're talking about those deliberate decisions and actions that break the rules because of a desire to achieve a certain end or condition. Can these decisions and actions damage what it means to be an Avenger and what the world may think of the Avengers? Is there a point where we can say that too many compromises have been made—and if so, how do we know where that point is?

Figuring Out the Rules

As Hank Pym indicates in the quote that begins this chapter, the Avengers have a duty to defend and protect the people of Earth from all manner of threats. This type of ethical framework, which judges the morality of an action by its adherence to rule-governed duty, is called *deontology*. In fact, adhering to a deontological framework seems to define what it means to be an Avenger.

Let's imagine a line: at one end we have the deontological rules the Avengers established to govern their actions, and at the other we have *consequentialism*. According to consequentialism, the morality of an action is judged by its overall results, such as maximizing the number of people who might survive a Skrull attack. Since we're imagining this as a line between two points, let's use one of Hawkeye's arrows as a marker to show where a particular viewpoint or decision falls between the two endpoints. If the world existed in only black and white, the arrow could just sit down at the deontological end and our heroes would never experience the tension of having to question their chosen rules. But the Avengers live in a world of at least four colors, so the arrow occasionally moves away from that endpoint, sliding along the line toward consequentialism, suggesting that the Avengers may have to compromise their duties for the sake of results.[3]

While the potential portfolio of decisions and actions that might move Hawkeye's arrow along our line is unlimited, let's focus on two in particular: secrets and lies. A secret is a piece of information that an individual or group doesn't want (some) others to know. A secret in itself can be considered amoral (neither moral nor immoral): no one would claim that you have to tell everyone everything (just think of birthday presents and surprise parties!). What matters morally is whom the information is being kept away from—and why. On the other hand, lying—intentionally giving someone false or distorted information—is inherently deceptive and therefore usually presumed to be immoral. It is no surprise that lies and secrets both travel in the same circles, with lies often being told to protect secrets. While lying is usually considered wrong, there are situations where it can fit within the deontological framework in which the Avengers operate: for example, placing brainwashed assassin-trained teenagers into new identities as part of a witness relocation program.[4] As with a secret, the victim and motivation of a lie are often of critical importance.

Occulting the Truth

Several years ago in the Marvel Universe, the US government passed the Superhuman Registration Act, requiring all super-heroes to register and reveal their secret identities, resulting in a "Civil War" that raged between Iron Man's pro-registration forces and Captain America's underground resistance.[5] During all of this, Doctor Strange, the dimension's Sorcerer Supreme, did his best impersonation of Switzerland: he went some-where snowy and meditated.[6] Wanting nothing to do with the violence that was about to rip the superhero community apart, Strange had his "arrow" well at the deontological end of our ethical spectrum. Participation in the events surrounding the registration act, on either side, would have been a viola-tion of his duties. But Strange could not stay neutral forever. The political storm calmed down a bit, Captain America was (apparently) killed, and a team of "New" Avengers broke from Tony Stark's team. At that point, he decided he needed to move that marker a little closer to the consequentialist end of the line, and so he stepped back into the fray to provide assistance to the New Avengers working covertly to fight crime and evil.

To help those Avengers on the lam, Doctor Strange offered sanctuary, disguising his house as a new location for a chain coffee shop.[7] As a result, villains, other heroes, and even other magic users did not know that the New Avengers were head-quartered at Chez Strange. Why did he do this? Because he decided that the law, and methods for enforcing it, were mis-guided at best and unjust at worst. In response he created a lie: the deception that his Sanctum Sanctorum had gone away, replaced by a purveyor of hot beverages. The consequence of conducting this deception was that the New Avengers were able to continue to fight crime and injustice.

This lie targeted everyone, be they licensed personnel from the Superhuman Registration Act, S.H.I.E.L.D. agents, common criminals, or just folks walking down the street—

and that is why we run into difficulty with this action. On behalf of the rest of the New Avengers, Doctor Strange lied to the same people whom he was sworn to protect: the general public. It's easy to say that "he had to do it," but we should be uneasy with what he did just as we are uneasy when our elected leaders in the real world keep things from their constituents—it may be justified, but he needs to explain why. Doctor Strange, and the New Avengers who benefited from his support, felt that this was an acceptable deception, given the context of the Superhuman Registration Act. But as we'll see, this decision had secondary effects on Strange that complicated things.

Sorcerer Supreme Emergency

Before we consider the effects on Doctor Strange, however, we need to discuss contemporary philosopher Michael Walzer's *supreme emergency*. According to Walzer, a supreme emergency is a justification for acts of war that would normally be in violation of just war tradition practices and the norms of the society fighting in a war, especially deontological rules that limit such actions. The *just war tradition* (or *theory* if you happen to be wearing a lab coat) establishes criteria for entering into and conducting a war in an ethical fashion. Over the centuries, the just war tradition has evolved to address both philosophical and theological concerns. For our purposes, the bottom line is that the just war tradition helps societies keep track of how far they might be moving Hawkeye's arrow from its deontological home toward the consequentialist end of the spectrum in times of war.

The example scholars normally use to illustrate the supreme emergency centers on the Allied bombing of Germany during World War II. As the standard argument goes, democracy (in the form of the United Kingdom) faced an existential threat from Nazi Germany. In response, Allied forces conducted bombing operations that may not have been in complete accordance with the just war tradition. The United Kingdom was in a state of supreme emergency, and a strict policy of maintaining the country's values could lead to utter destruction. So a temporary deviation from accepted norms was justified because it allowed the country—and its values—to continue once the emergency had passed.[8] These days, the most discussed example is the "ticking time bomb" rationale for using torture to extract secrets from a terror suspect. The purported justification is the same: compromising treasured values in the short term to ensure the persistence of those same values over the long term.

Of course, Walzer himself recognizes that it can be difficult to understand when the emergency has passed, and more importantly that it can become much easier to simply declare other supreme emergencies in order to justify deviating repeatedly from accepted norms.[9] This is not to say that these decisions form a slippery slope. We simply don't want hard decisions to become easier in the future. The challenge posed by adhering to a deontological framework is that it is not enough simply for a country to survive. The country must also be worthy of surviving. And that worth comes from adherence to the same values the country may be forced to compromise.

Doctor Strange highlights this danger by tripping down this path. He declared an emergency for the New Avengers due to how the Superhuman Registration Act was being enforced. He threw in his lot with them and lied to the entire world in support of their efforts. As physical and mystical pressure on his deception grew, he relied, against his better judgment, on ever greater and darker powers. With "World War Hulk," which began after the Hulk returned from his imposed exile in space (which a certain Sorcerer Supreme endorsed), Strange finds himself in yet another supreme emergency. This time we find him relatively at ease with moving the arrow all the way to the consequentialist end of the spectrum. Though he does try other tactics at first, he does not hesitate too long before giving himself over to possession by a demon to drive the Hulk off the planet.[10] At this point, the Eye of Agamotto determines that Strange has so violated the norms for Sorcerer Supreme that he is no longer fit to claim the title or associated power.[11] The compromises have been too much, and Dr. Stephen Strange himself is no longer worth saving as the Sorcerer Supreme.

Shhhhh—Avengers Assemble (in Secret)!

Secrets are not necessarily immoral, but how you protect them may cross a line (or move the arrow along one). After all, the founding Avengers recognized that some things must be hidden from the public view: the charter states that no Avenger may be forced to reveal their civilian identity.[12] Some have, of course: Clint Barton, Hank Pym, and Luke Cage, to name a few. But most try to keep that sort of thing on the down low. There are legitimate reasons for this, such as to protect loved ones and to allow some sense of anonymity when not in costume. With the exception of J. Jonah Jameson, there aren't many who would argue against the need for superheroes to keep this secret from the general public or even fellow teammates. (Even the supporters of the Superhuman Registration Act did not want to make secret identities public.) But there are always larger secrets.

The first five Avengers banded together to protect all mankind and allow Earth's inhabitants to meet "its rightful destiny." That's a very noble cause that few would argue against; if there were a real-world organization like this I know I'd be a big supporter. But let's play devil's advocate for a minute: who asked them to do this on the world's behalf? Technically, no group of individuals, states, or other political body asked them; it just seemed like a good idea at the time. Because they have done these good deeds in a generally transparent fashion, the Avengers have maintained the goodwill of the man or woman on the street and most political bodies around the world.

So why did they recently decide that they need a covert team that is kept a secret from the rest of the world and even other Avengers?

After the Siege of Asgard ended Norman Osborn's "Dark Reign" and ushered in the beginning of Marvel's Heroic Age, Steve Rogers undertook the enormous task of restructuring the Avengers. He handpicked the primary team (the Avengers) and the leadership of the New Avengers, established Avengers Academy to train young heroes, and created a special operations team, the Secret Avengers—led by Rogers himself.[13] His vision for the Secret Avengers was to conduct clandestine and undocumented activities against threats to the human race, preferably in a proactive fashion before the threats get out of hand.[14] Just as with Doctor Strange, there is a great deal of potential here to damage what it means to be an Avenger through overuse or misuse of secrecy and the steps taken to protect it.

The world knows of the Avengers, the New Avengers, and even Avengers Academy. Yet everything about the Secret Avengers is kept from the general public: the roster, the capabilities, the missions, and the very existence of the team. In battle, the team takes extra precautions to make sure that evidence of their presence isn't left behind.[15] There are several reasons for this, such as preventing foes from understanding the capabilities used against them or knowing that they are even being pursued by the Secret Avengers. But does this really require such an intensive and highly protected level of secrecy?

According to the Avengers Charter the team is a "sanctioned peace-keeping force by . . . the United Nations," having authority to perform operations, activities, and actions in "all countries belonging or affiliated with the United Nations." This sanction has varied over their comics history, but it stands to reason that the Avengers must subscribe to the highest level of transparency among UN member states to continue to enjoy this privileged status. Within this context, it doesn't appear that the Secret Avengers are doing anything untoward.

Almost every society accepts the need to keep some secrecy regarding capabilities and plans to defend against threats. In democracies, decisions like these necessarily move Hawkeye's arrow a smidge closer to the consequentialist end, but are often accompanied by public debate about what should and shouldn't be secret and what is acceptable behavior by organizations that deal in secrets.

In other words, democracies usually create something that the Secret Avengers don't have: oversight. Mechanisms are instituted to ensure that Hawkeye's arrow doesn't slide any farther down the line without a deliberate and acknowledged assessment of risks, including security threats as well as risks to the country's values. The Secret Avengers may be conducting their business in a fashion that is admirable and acceptable to the general world population. But the fact that they have zero accountability and oversight means that when—not if—their existence is made public, there will likely be a negative impact to the reputation of the entire Avengers enterprise. Questions will start to emerge: What else are they keeping a secret? Are they using secrets to cover up their mistakes? And does their secrecy really protect our interests?

Being Wikileaked On

Things get interesting when an impostor posing as U.S. Agent steals and releases vast amounts of intelligence that the Secret Avengers and others were using to develop leads and plans in response to threats across the globe. The leaked intelligence shows that the Secret Avengers were soliciting information from a wide variety of nefarious characters about the activities and plans of criminals, terrorists, and supervillains. As Steve Rogers himself put it, "Some did it for the right reasons, some did it to evade imprisonment, some just did it for profit."[16]

The fake U.S. Agent justifies his actions based on the lack of oversight and accountability on the part of all the Avengers teams, not just the Secret Avengers. Arguing that the stolen information and the unsavory characters who provided it are proof of Avenger misdeeds, he calls for transparency and oversight. So were the Avengers wrong to leverage information given willingly, although secretly, by those they would normally fight?

True, the Avengers fight criminals and supervillains. But as the charter states, the trial and punishment of wrongdoers is left to governments, with the Avengers only assisting in the imprisonment if conventional capabilities aren't sufficient. There is nothing to say that the Avengers cannot interact with the villains in other ways. After all, some villains have been rehabilitated by becoming Avengers, such as Quicksilver, the Scarlet Witch, and Hawkeye.[17] And the charter does lay out that the Avengers will share information with law enforcement groups such as S.H.I.E.L.D. and the New York Police Department, as well as have security clearances granted by the US government, which we can safely assume enables them to interact with the US intelligence community.

Furthermore, the law enforcement and intelligence communities deal with unsavory characters (such as "snitches" and worse—politicians) as part of their daily activities. Law enforcement needs confidential informants, criminals or sketchy characters who are willing to talk to the police in secret about underworld activity. And the intelligence community needs individuals willing to betray their countrymen and comrades by providing secrets to another state. The ethical arrow does move toward consequentialism, of course, but this is widely judged to be acceptable and necessary, provided there is oversight and some high-level degree of transparency—both of which the Secret Avengers lack. If sentiment ever turns against them, they will be in trouble.

"This Is the Kind of Thing That Is Going to Bite Us in the Butt"[18]

For the Avengers, adhering to the standards set by the founding members and the expectations of the people they protect can be difficult. Sometimes rules need to be broken to make sure the primary mission—protecting the human race—is accomplished. Within the much more narrow scope of secrets and lies, the standards can be even more difficult. There is the very real possibility that through their actions the Avengers may destroy what makes them the premier superhero organization of the Marvel Universe and keeps them admired by the world at large. And even when they may be working within the acceptable norms and rules, the mere perception that they're not can be just as dangerous.

This tension serves as a significant warning to those of us in the real world who are confronted by decisions that tempt us to compromise our values in favor of consequentialism. A reputation for honesty and integrity that is earned over a lifetime of heroism can be destroyed with a single decision—so make sure you have a good reason for it. (And that's no secret.)

NOTES

1. *Mighty Avengers* #24 (June 2009), reprinted in *Mighty Avengers Vol. 5: Earth's Mightiest* (2009).

2. For more on the Dark Avengers, see the chapter by Robert Powell titled "The Self-Corruption of Osborn: A Cautionary Tale" and the chapter by Sarah Donovan and Nick Richardson titled "Shining the Light on the Dark Avengers" in this volume.

3. Where Hawkeye's arrow may seem to go astray is *rule utilitarianism*, which recommends that people follow rules that are designed to produce the best consequences on the average. This is often put forward as simpler to follow, based as it is on established rules of thumb ("do not lie"), compared to *act utilitarianism* (the "normal" kind), which requires new considerations each time an ethical dilemma comes up ("will lying this time be okay?"). A problem with rule utilitarianism, however, is that it seems counterproductive to follow a rule even when you determine it won't produce good consequences—and since this is always possible, act utilitarianism would always be required anyway.

4. *Captain America and the Secret Avengers* #1 (May 2011).

5. *Civil War* (2007), collecting the seven-issue *Civil War* miniseries (2006–2007).

6. *Civil War* #6 (December 2006).

7. *New Avengers*, vol. 1, #28 (May 2007), reprinted in *New Avengers Vol. 6: Revolution* (2007).

8. See Michael Walzer, *Just and Unjust Wars: A Moral Argument with Historical Illustrations*, 4th ed. (New York: Basic Books, 2006), 251–254.

9. Ibid., 260.

10. *World War Hulk #4* (November 2007), reprinted in *World War Hulk* (2008).

11. *New Avengers*, vol. 1, #54 (August 2009), reprinted in *New Avengers Vol. 11: Search for the Sorcerer Supreme* (2009).

12. For a text of the Avengers Charter, see http://marvel.wikia.com/Avengers_Charter.

13. *Avengers*, vol. 4, #1 (July 2010), reprinted in *Avengers by Brian Michael Bendis Vol. 1* (2011).

14. *Secret Avengers #1* (July 2010), reprinted in *Secret Avengers Vol. 1: Mission to Mars* (2011).

15. *Secret Avengers #8* (February 2011), reprinted in *Secret Avengers Vol. 2: Eyes of the Dragon* (2011).

16. *Secret Avengers* #12.1 (June 2011), reprinted in *Fear Itself: Secret Avengers* (2012).

17. For more on the Avengers and rehabilitation, see the chapter by Andrew Terjesen titled "Cap's Kooky Quartet: Is Rehabilitation Possible?" in this volume.

18. Spider-Man, in *New Avengers*, vol. 1, #52 (June 2009), reprinted in *New Avengers Vol. 11: Search for the Sorcerer Supreme*.

THE AVENGERS
AND S.H.I.E.L.D.:
THE PROBLEM
WITH PROACTIVE
SUPERHEROICS

Arno Bogaerts

The last decade has been one of the most eventful and tumultuous periods in Marvel history. Among other things, the Avengers disassembled and reassembled into several splinter teams, the mutant population was decimated, a major civil war split the superhero community in two, a severely pissed-off Hulk warred against the world, the alien shape-shifting Skrulls staged a secret invasion, and Norman Osborn initiated a dark reign along with a secret cabal of supervillains. Through all these events, two major organizations in the Marvel Universe played important roles: the Avengers, Earth's primary and arguably most visible team of superheroes, and S.H.I.E.L.D., the international espionage, law enforcement, counterterror-ist, and global peacekeeping agency.

As Earth's Mightiest Heroes, the Avengers face threats no single superhero can withstand. They essentially react to and deflect the dangers posed by intergalactic and time-traveling conquerors, supervillain breakouts, and interplanetary wars. S.H.I.E.L.D., on the other hand, maintains a much more pro-active approach toward tackling global terrorism, conducting international espionage, and easing political tensions. While S.H.I.E.L.D. has always maintained close ties to Marvel's superhero community, in recent years it has become much harder to define what exactly sets them apart, with both Iron Man and Captain America in charge of S.H.I.E.L.D. at differ-ent times. In this chapter, then, we'll explore the dangerous slippery slope that can occur when superheroes use their pow-ers and influence in a proactive manner.

The Ultimates, the Avengers, and Nick Fury's S.H.I.E.L.D.

Nick Fury is a World War II veteran, a former CIA agent, and a superspy. As his prominent role as director of S.H.I.E.L.D., he served as the de facto liaison between the United States, the United Nations, and the superhero community. In fact, in the Ultimate Marvel continuity—a darker and more real-istic reimagining of the mainstream Marvel Universe—Fury's commanding presence can be felt in nearly every published story. There, S.H.I.E.L.D. was responsible for bringing the Avengers (or as they're known, the "Ultimates") together in the first place. The team was initially founded in *The Ultimates* as a paramilitary superhero defense initiative answerable to Fury (looking suspiciously like actor Samuel L. Jackson) and, by extension, the US government.[1]

Both *The Ultimates* and its sequel *The Ultimates 2* give us a darker look at what would happen if patriotic super-soldiers, armored billionaires, Asgardian thunder gods, gamma-fueled giants, and size-changing scientists suddenly popped up in post-9/11 America. After Captain America rescues several American hostages in the Middle East, controversy quickly breaks out over the world's new favorite superhero team. Should the American government and S.H.I.E.L.D. use superhumans—or as they are rather ominously called here, "Persons of Mass Destruction"—in foreign affairs?[2] After several conflicts within the team, the remaining Ultimates are used preemptively to "cripple a nation" in the Middle East, completely obliterating its nuclear weapons stockpile.[3] This sets off a major international backlash, after which we learn that the enemies of the United States have formed their own superhuman team, the Liberators, which retaliates by mounting a vicious attack on Washington, D.C., crippling both the Ultimates and S.H.I.E.L.D. While the Ultimates eventually win the day, the Liberators' attack on the US capital stands as a good example of the massive retaliation the use of superheroes in preemptive strikes almost always brings.[4]

In the mainstream Marvel Universe, too, Nick Fury and S.H.I.E.L.D. often use superheroes in proactive missions. For example, in *Secret War*, Fury and the Black Widow (both a S.H.I.E.L.D. agent and an Avenger) discover that Lucia von Bardas, acting prime minister of Latveria, is supplying lesser-known supervillains and terrorists with advanced technology.[5] Determined to strike at von Bardas before she can mount a terrorist attack on American soil (and send a message to anybody with similar thoughts), Fury embarks on an unauthorized mission to overthrow the Latverian government. To get the job done as quickly and efficiently as possible, he puts together a surgical strike team, including Avengers Captain America, Black Widow, Luke Cage, Spider-Man, and Wolverine (without being totally honest with them, I might add). They succeed in bringing down von Bardas (along with most of Castle Doom), but exactly one year later, von Bardas retaliates by launching a massive supervillain attack on New York City. While Luke Cage is sent to the hospital after being attacked in his home, the other superheroes, along with the Fantastic Four, barely manage to eliminate the threat and save New York City. Afterward Fury, having lost the respect of almost the entire superhero community, is forced to retreat underground and is replaced as director of S.H.I.E.L.D. by Maria Hill.

Dire consequences such as these seem inevitable when superheroes are proactive. But Nick Fury, for all his close relationships with the superhero community (and his own supernaturally prolonged life), is not a superhero. In his directorial position and as a self-proclaimed "wartime general," he's forced to see the bigger picture.[6] To get his job done and save lives, he doesn't mind performing questionable or downright dirty deeds in the name of the greater good—and if that means the unethical use of superheroes, then so be it.

Red and Gold Helicarriers?

This may be fine for Nick Fury, but whenever superheroes are forced to deal with issues like real-world politics, red tape, preemptive strikes, or any other proactive use of their powers, things tend to get tricky. Take Tony Stark, for example, and his travails over the last several years of Marvel events, all of which demonstrate Tony's patented take-charge, proactive stance toward . . . well, everything.

Let's start with the Civil War: the superhero community was split in two over the Superhuman Registration Act, which forced individuals with superpowers to surrender their identities to the US government and become official state agents (under S.H.I.E.L.D.).[7] Stark initially opposed the idea but eventually made a pragmatic decision to spearhead the movement after passage of the law became inevitable. He led the pro-registration forces against his former ally and friend Captain America, who saw the law as a violation of basic civil liberties. After a long and bloody conflict that ended with Cap's surrender and incarceration (and eventually murder), Iron Man was given the proverbial keys to the Helicarrier—and he used them to start a training program for young (and registered) heroes, put a registered superhero team in every state (the Fifty State Initiative), and, together with Fantastic Four leader Reed Richards and fellow founding Avenger Hank Pym, implement several of their "100 ideas that could change the world."[8]

After Stark took charge of S.H.I.E.L.D. and a reconstituted Mighty Avengers team, it was revealed that he, alongside several other heroes in a proactive and clandestine group known as the Illuminati, had banished Dr. Bruce Banner (the Hulk) into space to prevent more destructive gamma-fueled rampages.[9] The Hulk's ship landed on a savage planet named Sakaar, but eventually the Hulk found his way back to Earth, along with his new gladiatorial friends, where the ensuing battle devastated New York City.[10] Finally, the imperialistic, shape-shifting alien race known as the Skrulls unleashed a full-scale invasion of Earth. This was made possible in no small part by the Illuminati's botched proactive mission of years before, during which Skrulls learned enough to abduct and impersonate many well-known heroes without detection (including Avengers Hank Pym and Spider-Woman).[11] Furthermore, because Tony networked all the technology used by S.H.I.E.L.D. and the Fifty State Initiative to his own Stark tech, the Skrulls were able to completely cripple all of Earth's defenses in one fell swoop.[12]

Although the Skrull Armada was eventually driven back by the heroes (though not until after the death of the Wasp, another founding Avenger), Tony was blamed for everything and became the "World's Most Wanted" fugitive. S.H.I.E.L.D. was transformed into H.A.M.M.E.R. and placed under the command of the psychotic former Green Goblin, Norman Osborn, after he took the kill shot on the Skrull Queen. Osborn was elevated to the status of public hero, and in the position of top cop he plunged the Marvel Universe into a "Dark Reign" that forced nearly all the former Avengers underground. Osborn created his own Avengers team, with supervillains assuming the mantles of heroes like Ms. Marvel and Hawkeye, while Osborn branded himself as the Iron Patriot and wore a spare Iron Man armor decorated with Captain America's flag motif.[13]

I Didn't Mean It, Honest

Through all of this, Tony Stark showed himself to be the most pragmatic and proactive hero in the Marvel Universe, taking charge when no one else would and then suffering the consequences, including the scorn and resentment of his fellow heroes as well as the broader public (and much of the comics fan base). Yet as a futurist inventor, CEO of a billion-dollar company, and even former secretary of defense, it's hard for him not to look at the bigger picture—just like Nick Fury. So does Tony really deserve the blame for the causal chain of events that started with his well-intended (if overreaching) actions during these last several years of cataclysmic Marvel crossover events?

Whenever a person performs an action, both intended and unintended consequences (or side effects) may occur. So philosophers ask: which of these effects is the actor responsible for? One answer is presented in the *doctrine of double effect*, which originated in the writings of the philosopher Thomas Aquinas (1225–1274) and was elaborated upon by modern philosophers like Philippa Foot (1920–2010) and G. E. M. Anscombe (1919–2001). Simply put, the doctrine of double effect states that it is sometimes morally permissible to promote a good end even if—unintentionally but foreseeably—serious harm will result from it. It is not, however, permissible to cause the same harm intentionally.[14]

Consider killing in self-defense as an example of the doctrine of double effect. If a person—let's call him Nick, for no reason at all—is being attacked with murderous intent by someone—oh, say, Baron von Strucker—it is okay for Nick to defend himself against the Baron with lethal force (if necessary). In such a case, Nick would be protecting his own life—the good end—and the death of von Strucker would be the foreseen but unintended consequence of Nick's promotion of that end. On the other hand, if Nick discovered that the Baron is plotting to kill him, it would be morally wrong for him to kill the Baron first, since that would be the intended action itself (and there are many other ways to thwart von Strucker's plans and save Nick's life). In both scenarios the consequence—one dead Baron—is the same, yet only the first act, killing in self-defense, is morally permissible, because it is an unintentional side effect of the ethical act of self-preservation.[15]

The doctrine of double effect makes an important distinction between consequences that are intended and those that are merely foreseen (but not intended). Still, the line between them is not always clear, nor is it always clear how to "know" whether a side effect was truly unintentional. Another thorny issue is the matter of determining just how many bad consequences we will tolerate in the pursuit of good ends before we say "enough." For the doctrine of double effect to be accepted and work effectively, there has to be proportionality between bad effects (the means) and good effects (the ends). Assuming neither Fury nor Stark intended any harmful consequences of their actions, the remaining issue is whether the good ends they were pursuing were enough to justify the negative results of their actions. With Tony, especially, this question divided much of the Marvel Universe during the period described above.

What if the doctrine of double effect does not endorse Tony's actions? Does this imply that he's responsible for the negative outcome of the recent Marvel events? We don't have time here to launch an in-depth discussion of causation and responsibility. Suffice it to say that even the great futurist Tony Stark couldn't accurately predict the massive consequences his actions would have on the Marvel Universe. Note also that many other people's actions were involved, and the farther down the "chain of causation" we get from Tony's actions, the less responsibility we can pin on him.[16]

This Changes *Everything*
(Until It Changes Back)

As Simon Williams (Wonder Man) points out to Captain America, on the subject of putting the Avengers back together as a global peacekeeping force,

> maybe it's one of those things that you can't see when you're right in the middle of it, but once you step back it couldn't be more clear. From my point of view . . . the superhero civil war, the mutant decimation, the Skrull Invasion, Norman Osborn . . . they all have one thing in common . . . they are all the Avengers' fault.[17]

Well, let's take Simon's suggestion and step outside the confines of the Marvel Universe for a minute. It really does seem that any time a superhero tries be proactive, it comes back to bite him on the Asgard, almost as if the genre itself is preventing proactive superheroing.

The concept of the "status quo" in superhero stories is hotly debated. One minute fans are skeptical of claims that the next big event comic "will change everything you know—forever," because things always seem to revert to normal before long; and the next minute, fans complain that creators stray too far from established, beloved continuity. They want characters to develop—yet never change! However, the retention of a certain recognizable status quo in superhero stories is not only something that the upper management of Marvel and DC mandate (to maintain the economic viability of their licensing revenues outside comics), it's something that's ingrained in the very concept of the superhero itself.

In *Super Heroes: A Modern Mythology*, comics historian Richard Reynolds writes that the superhero is, by definition, "battling on behalf of the status quo," which he sees as the workings and positive values of the society in which most superheroes operate.[18] This status quo is "constantly under attack" and thus needs a superhuman protector from the outside forces of evil that attempt to change it.[19] Reynolds's vision seems to follow what philosophers Robert Jewett and John Shelton Lawrence call the "American monomyth," a variation on the classical monomyth (also known as "the hero's journey"). The mythologist Joseph Campbell (1904–1987) proposed the classical monomyth as a universal narrative in which a hero "ventures forth from the world of common day into a region of supernatural wonder," where fabulous forces are encountered, a decisive victory is won, and the hero returns "with the power to bestow boons on his fellow man."[20]

Jewett and Lawrence transfer this focus on the individual hero to the community. Thus in the American monomyth:

> A community in a harmonious paradise is threatened by evil: normal institutions fail to contend with this threat: a selfless superhero emerges to renounce temptations and carry out the redemptive task: aided by fate, his decisive victory restores the community to its paradisiacal condition: the superhero then recedes into obscurity.[21]

This certainly sounds a lot a like the typical superhero story. Combined with Reynolds's comments that the status quo, this (slightly exaggerated but nevertheless positive) "paradisiacal condition" of the community, must be defended over and over again, the superhero keeps from fading into obscurity by simply taking on the next supervillain. His adherence to the

American monomyth thus implies that the superhero, and the genre in which he operates, is primarily reactive. Something needs to happen—the status quo needs to be threatened—before a superhero can jump into action.

But I Want to Help!

Does this mean that it's better for superheroes like the Avengers to just sit back in their headquarters and do nothing until a supervillain comes along and destroys a couple of nearby buildings (usually their headquarters itself)? Actually, yes, but we all know that *that's* not going to happen. Their world and ours is hardly a "paradise," and there's always work to be done. We don't necessarily have to agree with Tony Stark's plans to help people through his advanced technology or his proactive actions during the Civil War, but neither can we let our heroes stand idly by and do nothing.

In her criticism of the doctrine of double effect, Philippa Foot asked if there is a moral distinction between what we do and cause directly by our action, and what we simply allow to happen indirectly by not acting, otherwise known as the *act/omission* question.[22] In some cases, she argued, there isn't, such as when a man murders his children by giving them poison (an act) or by refraining from giving them food (an omission), both of which would be wrong (to say the least). In other cases, though, we would make a strict distinction between acting and allowing. Foot, in another example, stated that most of us implicitly allow people to starve in Third World countries. However, it's one thing to allow people to die in far-away nations, and quite another to send them poisoned food. According to Foot, "There is worked into our moral system a distinction between what we owe people in the form of aid and what we owe them in the way of non-interference."[23] She then compared this distinction with the one between positive and negative duties. *Positive duties* describe things we should do, such as helping others, while *negative duties* detail things we shouldn't do, such as hurting others. Foot noted that our negative duties almost always seem to be morally stronger than our positive ones. So violating a negative duty (by acting to kill someone, for instance) is often considered worse than violating a positive duty (by not acting to save someone in danger).

For superheroes, however, positive duties seem to be more important than negative duties. We all know from reading Spider-Man comics that "with great power comes great responsibility," and in most cases this translates to helping those in need wherever you can. Furthermore, Spidey's origin story presents a strong case for this. Uncle Ben would still be alive if only Peter Parker had performed an act: stopping the burglar (who later killed his uncle) when he had the chance. But for superheroes, the greater responsibility may lie in keeping others safe from their power. Look no further than the Hulk: his famous request to be left alone shows that he does not want his incredible power to hurt innocent bystanders. He's more concerned with preventing harm than helping others, and given his unique nature, this is perfectly understandable.

Whenever superheroes act too much on their positive duty to help the world around them, they become proactive. And according to comics historian Peter Coogan, this inevitably sets them on a slippery slope toward, in essence, supervillainy. This is especially the case whenever superheroes, as Coogan puts it, "move up into governance" and become institutional parts of the society they're trying to protect.[24] We certainly saw this slippery slope into supervillainy happen with Iron Man's demonized depictions throughout many Marvel series during the Civil War and his subsequent tenure as director of S.H.I.E.L.D. Other examples include Thor's tenure as "Lord of Asgard" and later "Lord of Earth," during which his interference on Earth eventually led to a tyrannical rule that required time travel to undo.[25] Consider also the Squadron Supreme (onetime allies of the Avengers), who assumed control of the United States and attempted to remake the nation into a utopia. Despite their best intentions, the "utopia" they created was more like a totalitarian regime.[26]

While acting on positive duties is certainly admirable, practically every time we see superheroes attempt to do it proactively on a larger scale, the reactive nature of the super-hero genre brings them crashing down hard. Especially in long-running ongoing narratives like the Avengers, the general status quo always seems to return. And even though the team has seen its roster change many times, their general mission and place in society should not change. As Reynolds states, "The superhero has a mission to preserve society, not to re-invent it."[27]

Captain America's Mighty S.H.I.E.L.D. . . . Well, Sort Of

After the incarceration of Norman Osborn following the Siege of Asgard, a newly "reborn" Steve Rogers appeared before the president of the United States and was given Osborn's former position as top cop of the free world: "We've seen the world according to Nick Fury . . . We've seen the world according to Tony Stark . . . And, Lord in heaven, we've seen the world according to Norman Osborn. Steve Rogers, Captain . . . I am asking you to answer the call." Steve accepts, adding, "But . . . I'm going to want to do it my way."[28] As Captain America, Steve Rogers has certainly proven himself time and time again as a capable leader, perhaps even the most capable superhero leader in the Marvel Universe. But will he too, just like Nick Fury and Tony Stark before him, succumb to the same proactive methods and trappings his new governing role provides?

With Steve at the helm, it certainly looks like a brighter tomorrow for the Marvel Universe. So far, he has been doing a much better job in his elevated position than Tony Stark or even Nick Fury before him. He has as yet only shown vague hints of proactive action—chief among them his formation of the black-ops military stealth unit the Secret Avengers—and might possibly be the best top cop the Marvel Universe ever had.[29] However, Fury recently told Steve that "you may be good at being me for a while . . . but you don't have the constitution for it long-term."[30] And he may be right: shortly after he became the "new Nick Fury," Rogers once again became the one and only Captain America, following the apparent death of Bucky Barnes, signaling a return to the status quo—some things never change indeed!

NOTES

1. *The Ultimates* #1–13 (March 2002–April 2004), reprinted in *The Ultimates: Ultimate Collection* (2010). The popularity of this version of Fury can also be felt in Marvel's recent movies, in which the character—played by Mr. Jackson, of course—makes consistent appearances throughout the Marvel movies leading up to the Avengers film itself.

2. *The Ultimates 2* #1–13 (February 2005–February 2007), reprinted in *The Ultimates 2: Ultimate Collection* (2010).

3. *The Ultimates 2* #6 (July 2005).

4. Before you say anything—yes, I know the events in *The Ultimates 2* were manipulated by Thor's mischievous adopted brother Loki behind the scenes, but his "gentle nudging" of events has no impact on the point I'm making here. (He didst not tell me to say that either, nope.)

5. *Secret War* #1–5 (April 2004–December 2005), reprinted in *Secret War* (2006). The Eastern European country's more well known monarch, Doctor Doom, was trapped in hell at the time due to the events of *Fantastic Four*, vol. 3, #500 (September 2003), reprinted in *Fantastic Four Vol. 2: Unthinkable* (2003).

6. *Secret War* #5 (December 2005).

7. The Civil War event spanned numerous tie-ins throughout the Marvel Universe but was mainly told in *Civil War* #1–7 (July 2006–January 2007), reprinted in *Civil War* (2007).

8. *Civil War* #7 (January 2007). Number 42, for example, was the Negative Zone prison used to incarcerate anti-registration heroes and villains, while number 43 was cleaning up the S.H.I.E.L.D. organization. Later, Reed Richards added idea #101 to the list: "Solve Everything" (*Fantastic Four*, vol. 3, #570, October 2009, reprinted in *Fantastic Four by Jonathan Hickman Vol. 1*, 2010). Now *that's* ambitious, proactive superheroing for you!

9. *New Avengers: Illuminati* one-shot (May 2006), reprinted in *The Road to Civil War* (2007). The Illuminati have been in existence since the Kree-Skrull War, and their

mission was described by Professor Charles Xavier as meeting in secret to "proactively change catastrophes from happening" (*Avengers*, vol. 4, #9, March 2011, reprinted in *Avengers by Brian Michael Bendis Vol. 2*, 2011).

10. *World War Hulk* (2008).

11. *New Avengers: Illuminati* #1 (February 2007), reprinted in *New Avengers: Illuminati* (2008).

12. *Secret Invasion* (2009).

13. *Dark Avengers Vol. 1: Assemble* (2009). For more on Osborn and the Dark Avengers, see the chapter titled "The Self-Corruption of Norman Osborn: A Cautionary Tale" by Robert Powell and the chapter titled "Shining the Light on the Dark Avengers" by Sarah Donovan and Nick Richardson in this volume.

14. For a concise summary of the doctrine of double effect, see Alison McIntyre, "Doctrine of Double Effect," *Stanford Encyclopedia of Philosophy*, http://plato.stanford .edu/entries/double-effect.

15. This also shows why *consequentialism*, the school of ethics that judges the moral worth of an action based solely on the consequences said action brings about, firmly rejects the doctrine of the double effect, since intentionality (or lack thereof) has no impact on the goodness of outcomes.

16. For an overview of Tony's actions and moral responsibility, especially during the Civil War, see Mark D. White, "Did Iron Man Kill Captain America?" in *Iron Man and Philosophy: Facing the Stark Reality*, ed. Mark D. White (Hoboken, NJ: John Wiley & Sons, 2008).

17. *Avengers*, vol. 4, #1 (July 2010), reprinted in *Avengers by Brian Michael Bendis Vol. 1* (2011).

18. Richard Reynolds, *Super Heroes: A Modern Mythology* (Jackson: University Press of Mississippi, 1994), 77.

19. Ibid.

20. Joseph Campbell, *The Hero with a Thousand Faces* (Princeton, NJ: Princeton University Press, 1949), 28.

21. Robert Jewett and John Shelton Lawrence, *The American Monomyth* (Garden City, NY: Anchor, 1977), xx.

22. See Philippa Foot, "The Problem of Abortion and the Doctrine of the Double Effect," in *Virtues and Vices and Other Essays in Moral Philosophy* (Oxford: Basil Blackwell, 1978), 19–32.

23. Ibid., 27.

24. See Peter Coogan, *Superhero: The Secret Origin of a Genre* (Austin, TX: Monkeybrain Books, 2006), 216. (See chapter 4 in general for an analysis of the proactive/reactive relationship between the superhero and supervillain.)

25. For this period, see *Thor*, vol. 2, #51–79 (September 2002–July 2004), reprinted in a series of trade paperbacks. Also, on the difficulties with time travel and "fixing" the past, see the chapter by Andrew Zimmerman Jones titled "Can Kang Kill His Past Self? The Paradox of Time Travel" in this volume.

26. *Squadron Supreme* #1–12 (September 1985–August 1986), reprinted in *Squadron Supreme* (1996).

27. Reynolds, *Super Heroes*, 77.

28. *Siege* #4 (June 2010), reprinted in *Siege* (2010).

29. *Secret Avengers* #1 (July 2010), reprinted in *Secret Avengers Vol. 1: Mission to Mars* (2011). See the chapter by Louis Melançon titled "Secrets and Lies: Compromising the Avengers' Values for the Good of the World" in this volume on the Secret Avengers and the ethical issues faced by the covert special-ops team.

30. *Captain America* #619 (June 2011), reprinted in *Captain America: Prisoner of War* (2011).

PART FIVE

WHAT KIND OF WORLD DO THE AVENGERS LIVE IN?

CAN KANG KILL HIS PAST SELF? THE PARADOX OF TIME TRAVEL

Andrew Zimmerman Jones

Jessica Jones: Is this a time travel thing? 'Cause I hate time travel things.

Iron Man: If it's Kang, it's a time travel thing.

Jessica Jones: See. That's why I hate Kang.[1]

Ever since H. G. Wells, time travel has been a staple of science fiction and its close cousin, superhero comics. In the Avengers canon, perhaps the best-known time traveler is Kang the Conqueror, a warlord from the thirtieth century whose attempts to gain a foothold in the earlier centuries have frequently put him in conflict with the Avengers. At various times, he has shown up not only in the identity of Kang, but

also as Immortus (the "Master of Time"), the Pharaoh Rama-
Tut, the Scarlet Centurion, and Iron Lad (the founder of the
Young Avengers). Kang's time-hopping manipulations of the
Avengers actually predate his own first appearance. In the second issue of *Avengers*, the Space Phantom attempts to turn the
Avengers against each other, resulting in the Hulk's departure
from the team. The Space Phantom is, of course, later revealed
to be a minion of Immortus, the more scholarly (and manipulative) incarnation of Kang.[2]

For nearly a century, scientists and philosophers alike have
seriously debated whether the laws of physics, metaphysics,
and logic permit time travel. The problem is that once you
allow time travel, logical inconsistencies come up, which eventually transform into contradictions, which then blow up into a
full-on time paradox and potential violations of physical laws.

The Science of Bending Time

Though our current scientific model of time is based upon
Albert Einstein's theory of relativity—a fact for which Hank
Pym will always be profoundly jealous—the strange, ephemeral
nature of time has been pondered for centuries. The philosopher and theologian Saint Augustine (354–430) mused, "What,
then, is time? If no one asks me, I know what it is. If I wish
to explain it to him who asks me, I do not know."[3] Augustine
resolved the conflict through an appeal to a supernatural creator, but that option is not, as a rule, available to scientists.
Scientific attempts to quantify the ephemeral nature of time
have tended to be tied to the regular activity of a physical
system, which is the basis for any sort of timekeeping device,
from an astronomical calendar to a water clock to the digital
chronometer in Iron Man's heads-up display.

Einstein, however, realized that this same regularity created
an issue. Let's say that you set up a simple clock that consists of a
light that points straight up. It fires a tiny pulse of light that hits

a mirror one meter above it, and is then reflected back down to a detector right next to where the laser was emitted. Each cycle is a "tick" and a certain number of ticks indicates a second, and so on. One of Einstein's greatest insights was the realization that light moved at a constant speed, so this sort of ideal clock will be perfectly precise.[4] If you keep such a clock with you, you'll always have a precise measurement of the time wherever you are.

Unfortunately, there is a problem, which becomes evident if you consider the clock in motion. And there's no one better to choose when discussing motion than Pietro Maximoff, Quicksilver, although even he can't move fast enough for our example without some help. So let's assume that Quicksilver is traveling to the Shi'ar homeworld with his wife, Crystal. He sets sail on his fiftieth "birthday," in March 2014 (based on the first appearance of Quicksilver and his twin sister, the Scarlet Witch, in March 1964's *X-Men* #4).

Though the ship they're using should have faster-than-light engines, the engines are broken, and so Pietro and Crystal are forced to travel at a speed that is very fast, but still a bit shy of the speed of light. They decide the trip isn't worth the trouble and turn around, but they're moving so slowly (in cosmic terms, that is) that the trip still takes a while. Quicksilver is impatient, so he pays close attention to his clock, measuring exactly 365 twenty-four-hour periods (days, if you will) between his departure and his return. He shows up on Wanda's doorstep, ready to celebrate his fifty-first birthday!

Pietro's sister Wanda has a clock of her own, though. (Perhaps the matching set was a gift from dear old Dad, Magneto—the master race of mutants must be punctual, after all.) If she were able to use her hex powers to keep an eye on Pietro's clock while he was traveling, she would not see a stationary clock, but rather a clock in motion. In fact, while Pietro watches the light pulse travel only two meters (one meter up and one meter back down), Wanda sees the clock also travel almost two meters (remember, the ship's speed is just shy of light speed) in the horizontal direction. From Wanda's viewpoint, the pulse of light traces out two sides of an isosceles triangle with a height of one meter and a base distance just shy of two meters.

It doesn't take Hank Pym or Tony Stark—just some basic geometry—to figure out that the path of light Wanda sees is going to be longer than the path that Pietro sees. Since the speed of light is constant, it takes longer for the clock to complete a tick for Wanda than it does for Pietro. In other words, time on the spaceship moves slower than it does back on Earth.

For the sake of this example, let's say that Quicksilver's clock on the ship is moving at one-twentieth the rate of Wanda's clock. If the entire round trip took exactly one year according to Quicksilver's clock, Wanda's clock would say that it took twenty years. Here is the paradox: how old is Quicksilver upon his return? His birth certificate and driver's license indicate that he was born in March 1964 and he returns in March 2034, Earth time, so it would appear to be his seventieth birthday. But from his perspective, it's his fifty-first birthday. (Of course, in the case of Pietro, we run into further problems based on his superspeed metabolism and various aging issues related to extraneous time travel, but for the sake of this example, those can be ignored, as can his timeless Steve Martin–like hair color.)

What's intriguing about this example is that, mutant superpowers aside, it's completely consistent with the known laws of physics. In fact, it's a classic case known as the *twin paradox* (appropriately enough). The only reason we don't regularly run into this problem is the engineering challenge of building a near-light-speed spaceship. But smaller-scale experiments, such as those involving the lifetime of unstable particles before they decay, have absolutely confirmed this effect as predicted by Einstein. So it's not just an imagined effect of our hypothetical clocks. Real physical systems can actually experience time in different ways, depending on how they're moving relative to one another.

Breaking Time

The twin paradox is not really a logical paradox but rather an example of our normal language being unprepared for an unusual situation. Our intuition fails us, but there are no real scientific ambiguities. It's just a question of what point of reference should be used when defining aging. Nonetheless, it is a kind of time travel, in that it enables Pietro to travel ahead twenty years in Earth time while only aging one year himself.

For "real" time travel, the sort that allows Kang to shunt around the timestream battling the Avengers in ancient Egypt, the wild west, and modern-day Manhattan, the trip can't be one-way—he has to be able to travel back in time as well as ahead. So, is there any scientific way to travel backward in time? Actually, there are a few, in theory, at least (or perhaps I should say, at most).

To understand these theories, it's important to realize that Einstein's theory of general relativity describes a way to model how objects move within the universe once you've decided what that universe is like, based on parameters such as overall energy and matter density. The problem of defining the parameters of the theory and determining what weights to give them is an experimental challenge that physicists have been working on for nearly a century. On the bright side, these puzzles resulted in all sorts of unexpected findings such as dark matter and dark energy—okay, maybe not such a "bright" side—that aren't directly relevant to our discussion of time travel.

Time travel discoveries are of an entirely different sort, because they are (so far) mathematical discoveries only. Mathematicians and theoretical physicists tend to approach theories as if they're a *What If* comic book, creating hypothetical universes that fit certain criteria and then figuring out what the theories tell them about such a universe. This approach can result in some solutions that are mathematically feasible even though no experiment has ever revealed them. (This process,

in turn, gives experimenters some ideas of what to be looking for, so it's a useful exercise.)

For example, in 1937, physicist W. J. van Stockum asked us to imagine that there was an infinitely long cylinder spinning in empty space. When he used the mathematics of general relativity to analyze this hypothetical situation, he discovered that it was possible to have an object whose path started in one location in space and time and ended at the same location. (Such a path is called a *closed timelike curve*.) But unless you're visiting Galactus's barber (with the awesome power of the Silver Scissors), where are you going to find an infinitely long spinning cylinder?

In 1949, Einstein's friend and colleague, the mathematician Kurt Gödel, considered a more realistic scenario: what if the universe itself is spinning? Gödel discovered that such a universe—if it were spinning fast enough to avoid a collapse—would also result in closed timelike curves. Though Gödel himself was concerned about the possible paradoxes resulting from such a universe, there were two approaches to take in addressing those concerns: deny the physical possibility of the closed timelike curves, or deny the possibility of the paradoxes.

Einstein took the first. Since Gödel's model required a spinning universe, Einstein concluded that it probably didn't spin. (This tactic turned out to be valid because, to date, all evidence indicates that the universe is *not* spinning. Whew.) It's possible also to take the second approach, maintaining that time travel can exist, but that paradoxes cannot. On this view, the closed timelike curves create a loop, but the events on that loop are set in stone. If something happened in Kang's past and Kang goes back, then he was already there and he can't change what happened. The "future" Kang visiting his own past is also part of that past, and the events unfold in one and only one way, no matter what sort of time travel is involved.

Building a Time Machine

So we're left with our initial question: *could* Kang kill himself? Before we can explore that question in depth, we need to go one step further in the scientific realm: we have to build a time machine. In 1983, astronomer (and TV star) Carl Sagan sought help for his novel *Contact*, and in so doing contributed to a "realistic" notion for a time machine. To help, the physicist Kip Thorne came up with new solutions to general relativity that avoided a lot of problems but created entirely new ones.

The idea was built around a *wormhole*, which is a portal that opens in two locations and allows something going in one side to come out the other (like a tunnel). Such things are possible in physics (they're called Einstein-Rosen bridges), but they're believed to be highly unstable, one-way tickets and buried in the center of black holes (if they exist at all). To get around this, Thorne hypothesized having enough "negative energy" and "negative matter" to create a stable two-way wormhole. On paper this works, but in reality physicists don't have any reason to think that this stuff actually exists, and certainly not in the quantities needed to pull off this sort of stunt.

But let's assume that Kang has negative energy and matter in sufficient quantities to create a pair of movable portals that are connected by a wormhole. Kang leaves portal A on Earth, next to Wanda's clock, and he places portal B in Quicksilver's spaceship as he sets off on his journey. Portal B goes with Quicksilver and experiences a year of time, ending up in March 2034. On the other hand, portal A experiences a year of time and is in March 2015. Because the two portals are connected by a wormhole, this creates a portal between March 2015 and March 2034. This certainly seems like a far clunkier method of time travel than whatever Kang employs, but it allows him to implement a nefarious plan to destroy the Avengers once and for all.

In the next issue of this epic story arc, once Kang has his two time portals, he fires a laser into portal B. The beam comes out at portal A and gets deflected by mirrors for nineteen years until March 2034, when it reflects back into portal B along with the original laser. (Or, for the impatient, just put portal B thirty seconds into the future from portal A, which would give the Avengers less time to thwart the plan.) The beam entering portal B is now twice as powerful as the laser Kang initially used. But wait: because he's already got his mirrors all set up, the beam continues to bounce around and go into portal B yet again, resulting in a beam that is three times as powerful as the laser Kang initially used. If he does this over and over, he can end up with as much power as he needs to destroy the Avengers.

The problem is that Kang used a single laser to generate significantly more energy than he started with, which is a clear violation of the law of conservation of energy, one of the most important fundamental physical principles in our universe. It is this sort of problem that caused Stephen Hawking to propose a "Chronology Protection Conjecture." According to Hawking, since time travel allows for the violation of fundamental physical principles, there must be some law of nature that makes it impossible to actually build any sort of time machine: "The laws of physics conspire to prevent time travel, on a macroscopic scale."[5] This is essentially the same approach taken half a century earlier by Albert Einstein in response to Gödel's earlier closed timelike curve result: deny any potential physical reality to time travel. Not all physicists are convinced, however. Some continue to believe that time travel is consistent with the known laws of physics. Most of these physicists seem to think that the paradoxes are avoided because the closed timelike curves don't allow you to change the past, which is another way of making history safe for historians . . . or would-be conquerors.

Closed Timelike Kang

An entire volume could be written about Kang and time paradoxes—literary agents, you know where to find me—but I'll limit myself to three events from his checkered history that best show the immutable nature of closed timelike curves.

By the 1980s, all of Kang's time travel and manipulations had resulted in a lot of divergent timelines where Kang existed in various forms. One version of Kang (who is often called "Prime Kang") ends up in Limbo, from which he's able to see the various timelines and realizes that in many of them he is absolutely inept. So he sets a plan in motion to eliminate all of the "flawed" versions of himself "before the name of Kang becomes synonymous with 'fool'!"[6] The plan is mostly successful, but just as Prime Kang declares his victory, he discovers that he was manipulated by Immortus, the Master of Time, into eliminating all the extraneous Kangs. Driven insane by the memories of the Kangs he killed, Prime Kang vanishes into the halls of Limbo.

In this scenario, there is not just one path for Kang but many divergent paths, which seems to fly in the face of the idea of a closed timelike curve. The Marvel Universe is known to have many parallel worlds or universes, however. So the fact that variants of Kang exist isn't particularly troubling. Prime Kang himself explains this to the Avengers during the Destiny War: "Time-travel does not change the past—as I trust you've learned. If one alters the flow of events, it merely creates a new, divergent branch of the timestream, while the old one flows on."[7] In eliminating the "flawed" Kangs, Prime Kang has not altered the past (or even the future). Their actions already happened (or will already happen) in this timestream, but by killing them it just cuts down the overall number of Kangs running around.

From Kang's perspective, the problem is that he is destined to become the scholarly Immortus, which he views as a fate worse than death. He is Kang the Conqueror, after all, and the idea of giving up the conquering does not sit well with him. The effort to thwart this fate becomes Kang's motivation in the Destiny War. In this battle, Immortus seeks to not only prune the timeline, but to make changes that sweep through all timelines. He is successful in converting Chronopolis (Kang's cross-timeline base of operations) into the Forever Crystal to help him "change history—and reflect those changes throughout all of the timestream."[8]

In the final confrontation of the Destiny War, it is revealed that Immortus's various manipulations seem to have the goal of saving humanity from the wrath of his masters, the Time Keepers. In the end, Immortus is destroyed, which seems for a moment to shake even Kang's resolve. "They—killed him? Was that—my death, then?"[9] Instead, the battle ends when Captain America destroys the Forever Crystal, the effect of which splits Kang in two—Kang the Conqueror and Immortus—revealing that Immortus is not a replacement of Kang but rather a complete variant of him, a new worldline that branches off. He is able, through sheer chutzpah, to survive the creation of Immortus with his Kang identity still intact. The important thing to note is that Kang's attempt to change time to prevent the creation of Immortus is doomed to failure. Since he has encountered Immortus, it is inevitable that Immortus will eventually come into being; their individual closed timelike curves are set in motion and cannot be changed.

Finally, we see the same pattern at work with Iron Lad, a teenage version of Nathaniel Richards (Kang's true identity), who when confronted with the reality of the warmonger he will become flees to the twentieth century with Kang's armor.[10] Once there—or perhaps we should say "once then"—he gathers together a group of heroes, the Young Avengers, in an effort to stop the eventual, adult Kang. They succeed, in fact, but in doing so radically alter the timeline: Kang never exists because Iron Lad never becomes him, the Avengers are all dead, and the other Young Avengers begin to vanish from the timestream.

The only way to mend the timeline is for Iron Lad to accept his fate, erase his memories, and return to his own timeline so that he can ultimately become Kang.

In this case, again, we see that it's not possible to change the flow of events on this scale. When Iron Lad kills Kang, he creates a short-lived alternate timeline where Kang never existed, but this timeline is a closed loop that ceases to exist moments after it was created. Even if Iron Lad had stood fast in resolve, refusing to become Kang, there's no guarantee that years of living in desolation wouldn't eventually have led him to become Kang anyway. The timeline could have existed for twenty years, but the moment he became Kang, it would have ceased to exist and the original timeline would have popped back into existence.

Time to End

Physicists in our own reality may not be on par with Hank Pym or Reed Richards (yet), but they seem to have a better grasp than Kang does on how hard it is to change time. Stephen Hawking has said, when speaking of his Chronology Protection Conjecture, that "it seems there may be a Chronology Protection Agency at work, making the world safe for historians."[11] In the Marvel Universe, there is such a group: the Time Keepers and their minion Immortus. But when these powerful beings, or even just a gun-toting Kang, show up with plans to change time, it's the Avengers who step in to fill the role, to protect the timeline from harm. Even in a world where time travel is possible, there are still rules—and fortunately there are also Avengers to help enforce them.

NOTES

1. *Young Avengers* #2 (May 2005), reprinted in *Young Avengers: Sidekicks* (2006).

2. *Avengers*, vol. 1, #2 (November 1963).

3. Saint Augustine of Hippo, *Confessions*, trans. Albert C. Outler, 397, XIV 17, available at http://www.fordham.edu/halsall/basis/confessions-bod.asp.

4. Actually, this needs a vacuum, so assume the clock exists in a box that's had all the air removed.

5. Stephen Hawking, "Space and Time Warps," http://www.hawking.org.uk/index.php/lectures/63.

6. *Avengers*, vol. 1, #269 (July 1986), reprinted in *Avengers: Kang—Time and Time Again* (2005).

7. *Avengers Forever* #3 (February 1999), reprinted in *Avengers Legends Vol. 1: Avengers Forever* (2001).

8. Ibid.

9. *Avengers Forever* #11 (October 1999), reprinted in *Avengers Legends Vol. 1: Avengers Forever.*

10. *Young Avengers* #2.

11. Hawking, "Space and Time Warps."

"NO OTHER GODS BEFORE ME": GOD, ONTOLOGY, AND ETHICS IN THE AVENGERS' UNIVERSE

Adam Barkman

When Asgard, the home of the Norse gods, fell from the sky and landed in Oklahoma, one Christian pastor began his Sunday sermon by asking, "Small-g gods? Big-G? Are the Asgardians 'gods'? And if they are, well, where does that leave my God?"[1]

Though I feel for this pastor and his disrupted equilibrium, he actually has nothing to worry about. It's clear that in the Marvel Universe, God—capital "G"—exists. Doctor Strange learns about Him from the massive but not all-powerful cosmic being Eternity, who says, "I and my brother, Death, comprise all your reality! Neither he nor I am God, for God rules all realities!"[2] Thanos, even when he acquired the Heart of the Universe and bested the Living Tribunal (God's right-hand man), was naggingly aware of the Supreme Deity weaving the Titan's mischief for some higher purpose. "Was this my moment of triumph," he asked himself, "or but a facet of another's grand plan?"[3] As if that weren't enough proof, the Fantastic Four and Spider-Man have personally met Him: the Fantastic Four by entering Heaven itself and Spider-Man when God appeared as a homeless stranger to comfort the weary web-slinger.[4]

So God exists . . . but how do we reconcile this with the wide variety of beings in the Marvel Universe, including gods and demigods like Thor, Hercules, and Ares? Moreover, how should we understand the Marvel Universe in light of Exodus 20:3, which commands, "You shall have no other gods before me"?

God, the One-Who-Is-Above-All—or "Stan," for Short

In the Marvel great chain of godhood, God is the first-tier being and different from all other beings. He is the Creator, whereas everything else is creation. In three significant instances— in *Doctor Strange*, *Fantastic Four*, and, as the Fulcrum, in the *Eternals*—God is depicted as either Stan Lee or Jack Kirby, the literal creators of the Marvel Universe.[5]

In addition to being the Creator, God "is all-powerful and all knowing. It is the very essence of what holds reality in its place."[6] As such, God "sets the stage" for the drama of creation to play out.[7] Although God is transcendent and of a different category than all other Marvel beings, He is also immanent, interested and invested in what goes on in the realities He creates. "The play is your lives," He tells the Fantastic Four. "Your adventures become our exploration."[8] Just as an author has intentions as he writes, God has intentions—perfect intentions—in His creation. As He tells Spider-Man, "We all have a purpose, Peter. We all have a role to play."[9] That He is meant to be the Christian God is clear in the allusion to Jesus when He says to Peter, "And, you know, if it's any consolation, I've asked a lot more from people much closer to me than you."[10] Indeed, the Watcher tells the Invisible Woman, "His only weapon is love!"[11]

Below God in the Marvel great chain of being is the Living Tribunal, a mysterious figure. Like the "Living Creatures" of Ezekiel 1:6, each of whom has four faces, the Living Tribunal has four faces (three and a "void"),[12] and like the Living Creatures, who adore God in His throne room, the Living Tribunal is "the representative of The-One-Who-Is-Above-All."[13] The Living Tribunal's "task is to sit in judgment of events on the far end of the cosmic scale," with each of his three visible faces representing a mode of his righteous judgment: necessity, equity, and vengeance.[14] Each face can be likened to an angel in the Bible who pours out judgment in the name of the Most High.[15] Indeed, the Living Tribunal's face of necessity paraphrases Jesus when he tells She-Hulk, "Necessity is the Cosmic mirror which reminds us to always judge others as we would have ourselves judged."[16]

Below God and the Living Tribunal are the cosmic beings or astral deities of the universe. These include the Celestials, Lord Chaos and Master Order, the Watcher, Galactus, Love and Hate, Kronos, Eternity, and the Chaos King.[17] Most of these cosmic beings are involved in the birth or death of universes, yet none of them are absolutely indestructible or eternal; all suffer defeat at one time or another. Below the cosmic beings are the fourth-tier beings, the elders of the universe, who include the Collector, the Grandmaster, Chthon, Gaea (Mother Earth), and possibly Death.[18]

Of course, all this talk about tiers of beings only explains things such as longevity and parenthood. Those influenced by Greek philosophy and Judeo-Christian theology might maintain that that which is oldest is that which is strongest, wisest, and most indestructible. Plato believes this to be true of the Forms, and the Judeo-Christian believes this to be true of God.

We can't extend this to Greek and Norse polytheism, however. In both of these cases (not to mention in the case of one of their root sources, Mesopotamian mythology),[19] the late-coming sky fathers, Zeus and Odin, were able to defeat their respective fathers and claim supremacy even while the primordials lingered in the background. Likewise, in the Marvel Universe lesser beings such as Thanos (an Olympian god modified by the Celestials) can wield the Infinity Gauntlet, which in turn can defeat Eternity, and Hercules the sky father is able to best the Chaos King. Thus, in respect to created things in the Marvel Universe, order of existence is one thing that separates the cosmic beings, elders, and sky fathers even if not much else, absolutely speaking, does. *"Aztec"* *Mexican*

"Gods Are a Bit Different"

We should expect, then, that when we turn to look at the differences between "gods" and "nongods" among the Avengers, we won't find absolute differences. Take Thor, for instance. Gaea gave birth to the sky father Odin, the supreme god of the Asgardians, and together Odin and Gaea (in the guise of Jord) gave birth to Thor.[20] Odin apparently claims the title of sky father because he was directly (without the aid of a lower being) birthed by Gaea, an elder, whereas Thor is a lower god because his blood was diluted by having a sky father for a parent.

Most of the gods in the Marvel Universe, including the Asgardians, live in dimensions different from that of the Avengers, and they are able to intervene in the human dimension more easily than humans can in that of the gods. The gods' greater magical ability also seems to give them greater resistance to magical attacks. For example, although Lord Nightmare, who is a being roughly on par with the gods, was able to take control of "those with mortal minds," Thor, a god, remained unaffected.[21] The gods' strength also generally exceeds that of mortals, even superhuman ones. When Skaar, son of the

God means what X

Hulk, asks, "Gods? So what? We've fought every monster and demon," She-Hulk quickly replies, "You don't understand. Gods are a bit different."[22] And indeed, they are: "Among mortals," Hera tells the Hulk, "you may be the strongest one there is but Father Zeus could vaporize you with a thought." Although Zeus doesn't do that, he does soundly defeat the Hulk, chaining him up like Prometheus for vultures to pick at. In fact, even though Loki magically possesses the Hulk in order to turn him against Thor, saying, "Only you have ever brought near defeat to the mighty Thor,"[23] Thor, not the Hulk, can lift the magical hammer Mjolnir, and Thor, not the Hulk, emerges victorious. As the Wasp says on behalf of her fellow Avengers, "Thor, we already know you are the strongest."[24]

Of course, as with most everything in this graded but not rigidly fixed universe, these kinds of statements are general, not unqualified. For example, strength is an unclear term. Does it mean mere physical might or does it include, even leaving magic aside, other nonphysical abilities? Graviton's power over gravity, for instance, is sufficient to defeat Thor, and so he rightly asks, "Do you think I would surrender because of your supposed godhood? Perhaps I too am a god."[25] And even if for the most part gods are physically stronger than superhumans, a single god such as Hercules can be physically defeated by a group of lesser beings, which is exactly what happens when Mr. Hyde, Goliath, and the Wrecking Crew beat him to within an inch of his life.[26]

Ontology Comics #1

So what does it mean to be an immortal? In *ontology*, the area of philosophy that studies the nature of being or existence, we say an *eternal* being is "outside" of time, having no beginning and no end; an *immortal* being has a beginning in time but no end; and a *mortal* being has a beginning and end in time. In the Marvel Universe, only God is eternal. Because all other beings are creatures (that is, created by God), all other beings are either mortal or immortal. But because all creatures, except for Thanos and Adam Warlock, will have died (as shown in *Marvel Universe: The End* #6), it seems very likely that all creatures can die. Thus, strictly speaking, everything in the Marvel Universe is mortal except God.

Nevertheless, there is another sense in which not just the cosmic beings, elders, sky fathers, and gods but also superhumans, aliens, and humans can be thought of as immortal, or, in the words of Thor, "ever defying the eternal sleep."[27] The sky fathers Odin and Zeus, for example, have died multiple times, but they continue to endure, albeit in different forms, in their respective underworlds alongside, more important, the naked souls of mere superhumans and humans who have perished. All creatures are able to die, yet all (by God's decree, to be sure) are able to endure as well. Indeed, it's not unusual in the Marvel Universe for cosmic beings, elders, gods, and humans alike to be resurrected or reincarnated.[28] Thus when the gods are called "immortal" we should just take it to mean they can't die from old age or disease, not that their "physical" bodies can't perish.

The Hulk, the Wasp, and Black Widow are all on lower "levels" ontologically than the god Thor, although this is mostly in respect to lineage and age and only to a lesser extent in respect to natural immunities and abilities. All four, of course, were made by God via his servants Eternity and Gaea and in this respect are equals. But human beings, we are told, were given the finishing touches by the sub-sub-sub-subcreator Odin ("Some whisper that he made the first man").[29] If true, this would mean that whereas Thor, as the son of Odin, was *begotten* by Odin, the Hulk, the Wasp, and Black Widow were *created* (or touched up) by Odin.

So, given the existence of "one supreme" God (who says, "You shall have no other gods before me"), how can we make sense of all these other gods in the Marvel Universe? The term "god" (lowercase) is used in the Bible to describe nonexistent deities represented in statues (such as Dagon in 1 Samuel 5:4), rebellious angels (such as Satan), and even, importantly, human beings. Psalm 82:6 reads, "I said, 'you are gods'; you are all sons of the Most High"—a passage quoted and elaborated on in John 10:34, in which Jesus says:

> Has it not been written in your law, "I said, you are gods"? If he called them "gods," to whom the word of God came (and Scripture cannot be broken), do you say of Him, whom the Father sanctified and sent into the world, "You are blaspheming," because I said, "I am the Son of God"?

Therefore, other "gods" can coexist with the God of the Judeo-Christian tradition as well as with the God of the Marvel Universe.

Does Godliness Imply Goodness?

In the Marvel Universe, as in our own, ontological status—which generally goes hand in hand with order of creation, longevity, power, and knowledge—is no measure of moral goodness. We have Satan and Marvel has Mephisto: both are extremely old and powerful beings who happen to be evil. This isn't just true of the devils, however. When wearing the Infinity Gauntlet, Adam Warlock foolishly imagines that a proper supreme being must not permit "good and evil to cloud his judgment," and even his "good" aspect, the Goddess, is nothing of the sort, imagining that goodness is something that can be forced, rather than wooed.[30] Indeed, Galactus and the Celestials massacre millions when they destroy worlds; the goddess Hera shows her immorality when she tells the Hulk, "An oath to a monster means nothing"; and Eternity himself is at odds with God when he tells Dr. Strange, "I am above such petty emotions as gratitude!"[31] Power and privilege rarely, it seems, translate into right actions.

So how did evil come to be? Hints consistent with the basic Judeo-Christian story are found throughout the Marvel Universe. In *Fantastic Four*, vol. 3, #511, God tells the Four that they are His "collaborators," saying, "You're no one's puppets . . . Nobody can do your living for you," and in *Sensational Spider-Man* #40, when Peter asks God why he has been given his powers, God replies by showing him the scores of people he has saved along the way, saying, "They are some of the point, Peter." God creates because He loves to create, to be sure, but He creates rational beings ("gods" of all sorts) for communion with Him (or for them to commune with the Good) and to spread Goodness to others. Because good and evil only have meaning insofar as a person is free, God has given all His "gods" free will to choose between good (God) or evil. The true meaning of "you shall have no other gods before me," then, is not to deny the existence of other gods, but rather to love everything properly: God and goodness above all else. Evil creatures are simply those who value or elevate anything else above God the good and His moral laws. The wise understand this; thus the Watcher says to the Dreaming Celestial:

> The pulse that seemed to be completely random at first, but now registers with every cycle? That is what humans call a conscience. It's what recognizes and differentiates good from evil. It took me even longer to realize that the best thing to do was simply heed it.[32]

Although diverse and not particularly powerful in the grand scheme of things, the Avengers also understand this. For instance, Thor understands that the difference between right and wrong is important, and so he tells "the slayer of the gods," Devak, "I have long agreed that some gods are malevolent and dangerous. But your inability to discern between good and evil makes you equally as dangerous."[33] And although he is "not exactly humble" and at times rather brash, the God of Thunder loves the good as all heroes do.[34] More than this, however, he understands that justice is perfected or completed by love—indeed, by *agape* or sacrificial love, the supreme love, the love that the Bible claims is one of God's names.[35] Thor, as a lover of the good, loves justice (treating each as it ought to be treated) and mercy (going beyond, in a positive way, the commands of justice), saying, "I shall not falter in my resolve to protect this planet and save its people!"[36] And so he gives protection, even when faced with the terrible ethical dilemma of having to kill an innocent (the human time bomb that the Wasp became by the end of the Skrull invasion) to show this love.[37] All of the Avengers love the Good, and since the Good is an aspect of God, they can be said to love God either clearly or through a glass darkly.

Equal Opportunity—for Deities?

Duane Freeman, the representative of the American government to the Avengers, once tried to pressure the team into accepting more minorities into the team, to which Iron Man replied:

> We don't recruit for skin color. The Avengers aren't about equal representation—the squads are too small for that. We're about getting the job done—and that's it. We've had minority members for years—from black and Hispanic heroes to gypsies and mythological gods. We'd never exclude anyone—*anyone*—because of their race.[38]

Something similar is true of God, both in the Marvel Universe and our own. The Creator is pleased to accept not only human beings, but also any and all free-willed creatures ("gods") that He has made. He accepts them under one condition, however: they must love Him, and by that He means they must love the Good. In this way, the Avengers are a model for us all, for though they are diverse, they are unified in their love of Goodness itself—or Himself.

NOTES

1. *The Mighty Thor* #1 (June 2011), reprinted in *The Mighty Thor Vol. 1: Galactus Seed* (2011).

2. *Doctor Strange*, vol. 2, #13 (April 1976), reprinted in *Essential Doctor Strange Vol. 3* (2007).

3. *Marvel Universe: The End* #6 (August 2003), reprinted in *Marvel Universe: The End* (2011).

4. *Fantastic Four*, vol. 3, #511 (May 2004), reprinted in *Fantastic Four Vol. 4: Hereafter* (2004); *Sensational Spider-Man*, vol. 2, #40 (September 2007), reprinted in *Spider-Man, Peter Parker: Back in Black* (2008).

5. See *Strange Tales*, vol. 1, #157–163 (June–December 1967), reprinted in *Essential Doctor Strange Vol. 1* (2006); *Fantastic Four*, vol. 3, #511; and *Eternals*, vol. 4, #9 (May 2009), reprinted in *Eternals: Manifest Destiny* (2009).

6. *Eternals*, vol. 4, #9.

7. *Fantastic Four*, vol. 3, #511.

8. Ibid.

9. *Sensational Spider-Man*, vol. 2, #40.

10. Ibid.

11. *Fantastic Four*, vol. 1, #72 (March 1968), reprinted in *Essential Fantastic Four Vol. 4* (2006).

12. *Silver Surfer*, vol. 3, #31 (December 1989).

13. *The Infinity War* #2 (July 1992), reprinted in *Infinity War* (2006). Note that this "title" should not be confused with the Prime Celestial, The One Above All, who is a mere Celestial, a servant of the Fulcrum (*Thor*, vol. 1, #287, September 1979, reprinted in *Thor: The Eternals Saga Vol. 1*, 2006).

14. *The Infinity War* #3 (August 1992), reprinted in *Infinity War*.

15. Exodus 12, 2 Samuel 24:16, 1 Corinthians 10:10, Hebrews 11:28, and Revelation 9:11.

16. *She-Hulk*, vol. 2, #12 (November 2006), reprinted in *She-Hulk Vol. 4: Laws of Attraction* (2007).

17. It's not very clear how he differs from Lord Chaos.

18. In the old literature, Death is often depicted as Eternity's opposite, which would make him or her a cosmic being. However, during the Chaos War the Chaos King is depicted as Eternity's true opposite and Death is a clear subordinate. For the old version, see *Captain Marvel*, vol. 1, #27 (July 1973), reprinted in *Marvel Masterworks: Captain Marvel—Vol. 3* (2008); for the new version, see *Chaos War* #2 (January 2011), reprinted in *Chaos War* (2011).

19. In Mesopotamian mythology the second-tier god Ea kills his first-tier father—the primordial Apsu—and Ea's son, the third-tier god Marduk, slays the first-tier primordial goddess Tiamet to become the king of the gods. Enuma Elish 1.4, 1.69, and 4.104.

20. *Thor*, vol. 1, #300 (October 1980), reprinted in *Thor: The Eternals Saga Vol. 2* (2007).

21. *Chaos War* #2.

22. *Incredible Hulks* #622 (February 2011), reprinted in *Incredible Hulks Vol. 1: Chaos War* (2011).

23. *Hulk vs. Thor* (Marvel Animation, 2009).

24. *Avengers*, vol. 1, #220 (June 1982).

25. *Avengers*, vol. 1, #159 (May 1977), reprinted in *Essential Avengers Vol. 7* (2010). Also see *Avengers: Earth's Mightiest Heroes*, season 1, episode 7 (Marvel Animation, 2010).

26. *Avengers* vol. 1, #274 (December 1986), reprinted in *Avengers: Under Siege* (2010).

27. *Avengers* vol. 1, #277 (March 1987), reprinted in *Avengers: Under Siege.*

28. For example, see the Asgardians restored in *Thor by J. Michael Straczynski Vol. 1* (2008), after the events shown in *Avengers Disassembled: Thor* (2004).

29. *Thor*, vol. 2, #83 (October 2004), reprinted in *Avengers Disassembled: Thor.*

30. *The Infinity War #2; The Infinity Crusade #3* (August 1993), reprinted in *Infinity Crusade Vol. 1* (2008).

31. *Incredible Hulks* #622; *Doctor Strange*, vol. 2, #13.

32. *Eternals*, vol. 4, #9.

33. *Thor*, vol. 2, #78 (July 2004), reprinted in *Thor: Gods & Men* (2011).

34. *Avengers*, vol. 1, #220.

35. 1 John 4:8.

36. *Thor*, vol. 1, #388 (February 1988), reprinted in *Thor: Alone Against the Celestials* (1992). See also the 2011 film *Thor*, in which Thor tells Loki, "These people are innocent. Taking their lives will gain you nothing. So take mine and end this." And then, dying, we hear Thor say the words, "It is over," echoing the words of the dying sacrificial Jesus, "It is finished" (John 19:30).

37. *Secret Invasion* #8 (January 2009), reprinted in *Secret Invasion* (2009).

38. *Avengers*, vol. 3, #27 (April 2000), reprinted in *Avengers Assemble Vol. 3* (2006).

LOVE AVENGERS STYLE: CAN AN ANDROID LOVE A HUMAN?

Charles Klayman

Once upon a time, two Avengers, the Vision and the Scarlet Witch, had a romantic relationship that led to marriage. Several of their fellow Avengers were skeptical because, after all, Vision is an android and the Scarlet Witch is a human (more precisely, a mutant, but that distinction isn't relevant here). Whether made of synthetic or organic components, androids are artificial and not what we would call "alive." But they can look amazingly similar to us (without the love handles and blemishes) and can seem self-aware, as if they have conscious existence similar to our own. So, given their differences and similarities, can an android love a human (and vice versa)?

What Is Love, Anyway?

Inspired by Plato and Aristotle,[1] the philosopher and Christian apologist C. S. Lewis (1898–1963) categorized four general types of love, which are *affection, friendship, Eros* (or romantic love), and *charity*.[2] For Lewis, each type of love contains three qualities or elements, which are *gift-love, need-love*, and *appreciative-love*. Different types of love might contain unequal portions of elements, and while these elements seem separate from each another, they actually "mix and succeed one another, moment by moment."[3]

The most basic *need-love* often runs the risk of being interpreted as selfishness. We don't call a toddler selfish when he grasps for his mother with outstretched hands. The toddler simply displays love, which happens to manifest as a need for his mother. Need-love is seen in relation to our own needs and will not last longer than the need; once the mother has picked up the toddler, the toddler's need has been fulfilled. Yet not all needs are transitory: "The need itself may be permanent or recurrent."[4]

On the other hand, *gift-love* implies giving—not necessarily out of the goodness of one's heart, but from the need to give. The mother doesn't give attention to her toddler because she's a nice person, but because she needs to give to her child. With gift-love, the person longs to give her beloved happiness, comfort, protection, and so forth.[5]

Finally, rather than giving or receiving, *appreciative-love* involves "judgment that the object is very good, this attention (almost homage) offered to it as a kind of debt, this wish that it should be and should continue being what it is even if we were never to enjoy it, can go out not only to things but to persons."[6] So when I say, "I love my weekly pizza night," I mean that I judge that pizza is such a good thing that I reserve a time once a week not only to savor it but to admire all its qualities and hope that after my demise the institution of pizza-making will continue.

Friends, Lovers, and Significant Others

How do these aspects combine to form the different types of love, and which one best applies to the Vision and the Scarlet Witch? First, let's consider *affection*, which is based on familiarity. Clearly, eating pizza once a week becomes a familiar routine, and often things that we grow accustomed to are things that we grow to love. It is also from this type of love that jealousy comes into play: "Change is a threat to Affection."[7] Change my Friday night pepperoni pizza to a sushi platter and witness how I'll fight to reclaim my pizza night. Change the toddler into a rebellious adolescent and listen how the mother asks what has become of *her* baby. It seems that a human could grow accustomed to an android over a period of time, yet affection does not seem to be the type of love that the Scarlet Witch had for the Vision. Obviously, as an Avenger, she grew affectionate toward him, especially since they knew each other for thirty-two issues before they became involved romantically.[8] While a human can have affectionate love toward an android, affection alone is not enough to pursue a romantic relationship or marriage.

Might friendship be enough to generate the Vision and the Scarlet Witch's love? While the Avengers are a team, it seems as teammates they would be companions but not necessarily friends. For example, after a hard day of combating evil, we might imagine Wonder Man and the Beast partying away the night together, yet I doubt they would invite Captain America or Hawkeye to join their festivities. They might think these two are excellent teammates and Avengers, but they probably wouldn't want to spend their leisure time with them. After all, Captain America is too goody-goody and Hawkeye is a jerk.

Not wanting to spend leisure time with a fellow Avenger might not seem right, but Lewis uses the terms *friendship* and *companionship* in very specific ways. Friendship is another type of love, while companionship is not. Whereas friends are necessarily companions, companions do not necessarily rise to the level of friends. Companionship arises out of the instinct to cooperate, but friendship arises "out of mere Companionship when two or more of the companions discover that they have in common some insight or interest or even taste which the others do not share and which, till that moment, each believed to be his own unique treasure (or burden)."[9] The commonality that inspires friendship often manifests as a common vision or a shared way of seeing and caring about the same truth.[10] The Avengers, for example, might be friends with one another insofar they share the same interest of defeating villains and have the same vision of good triumphing over evil.

Given Lewis's handling of *friendship*, it seems that a human can love an android as a friend. The Scarlet Witch and the Vision are more than friends, however, especially once they declare their love for each other.[11] To be "more than just friends" often implies a type of love that is romantic, which Lewis calls *Eros*, the state of being in love.[12] This type of love is often associated with a type of sexual desire, which Lewis names *Venus* to contrast it from, for example, the type of sexual desire that animals experience. From an evolutionary viewpoint, Eros develops out of Venus, but Lewis argues that Eros doesn't begin from a physical state. Rather, it begins from a mental state—preoccupation. "A man in this state really hasn't leisure to think of sex. He is too busy thinking of a person. The fact that she is a woman is far less important than the fact that she is herself."[13]

Lewis is saying two things here. First, romantic love does not develop primarily from sexual desire, but rather from fascination. Second, the beloved is a *self*, which is admirable and unique. This self lurks behind one's physicality; it is the inner person, soul, or the "real you." As Lewis says, "Now Eros makes a man really want, not a woman, but *one particular woman*."[14] So the romantic lover is in love with a specific, unique individual who cannot be replaced.

The lover sees his beloved as something that is good, independently of any pleasure or happiness that the beloved gives to the lover. The point of Eros is to become one with the beloved. Romantic couples are, as we say, "an item"; whereas friends stand side by side, lovers stand face to face.[15] As Lewis says, "One of the first things Eros does is to obliterate the distinction between giving and receiving."[16] In cases of true Eros, the line between giving and receiving vanishes.

Unreciprocated Love

Is it still Eros, though, if the beloved is unwilling or incapable of standing, as it were, "face to face" with the other person? Perhaps, but it would be an unhealthy Eros. Suppose that She-Hulk has a crush on Jarvis, the Avengers' butler, who ignores her, unwilling to reciprocate her love. Captain America might advise her, "Keep at it! Jarvis is bound to come around," yet Wonder Man might say, "Give it up! He'll never go for someone like you." That's often the kind of advice we get when we find ourselves in a similar situation: either keep at it until the beloved notices the real us and returns our love or else give up our fascination and preoccupation with the beloved.

Consider the Greek myth of Narcissus, who fell in love with his own reflection. Obviously his reflection was unable to return his love, and poor Narcissus died, unable to leave his own reflection. As in the case of She-Hulk and Jarvis, if love is not reciprocated it can become an obsession or craze. So it seems that a human can romantically love an android, but if the love is not reciprocated it is unhealthy.

While Eros might be unhealthy if it is unreciprocated, for Lewis, there is a type of love that involves loving the unlovable.

As paradoxical as it sounds, Lewis relies upon the idea of the Christian God in order to explain the fourth type of love, *charity*, which is essentially an expansion of gift-love. Lewis makes a distinction between natural gift-love and a share of God's own gift-love, which he classifies as *divine gift-love* and *Love-Himself*.

> Natural Gift-love is always directed towards objects which the lover finds in some way intrinsically lovable—objects to which Affection or Eros or [Friendship] attracts him. . . . But Divine Gift-love in the man enables him to love what is not naturally lovable; lepers, criminals, enemies, morons, the sulky, the superior and the sneering. Finally by a high paradox, God enables men to have a Gift-love towards Himself.[17]

There seems to be a problem with giving to God since everything is already His, but for Lewis, we can give to God by being kind and charitable: "Every stranger whom we feed or clothe is Christ. And this apparently is Gift-love to God whether we know it or not. Love Himself can work in those who know nothing of Him."[18] Charity is a love where the beloved is not one particular person but rather people in general. So a human could love an android out of charity, but such a love would not be limited to that one particular android.

"No Sister of Mine May Become Involved with a—a—a Robot!"[19]

It seems that a human can love an android whether that love is affection, friendship, Eros, or charity. Yet Eros seems to be what best describes the relationship between the Scarlet Witch and the Vision. So now we need to determine if an android can love a human in a similar fashion.

We might think that androids are incapable of love because they are machines, like circular saws and blenders.

This argument has a subtle problem, though. It assumes that only humans can love. Obviously this is false, since nonhumans such as Thor or Mar-Vell can love. Still, they're alive, whereas machines are not. Clearly some machines, such as the mutant-hunting Sentinels, are incapable of love. In a way, though, humans are "flesh machines," composed of organic components and programmed by a genetic code, operating in response to environmental stimuli. So not all machines are incapable of love.

Perhaps humans and nonhumans, like Thor and Mar-Vell, are *persons*, whereas androids are not. And perhaps only persons are capable of love. The problem with this line of argument is that personhood is a vague concept. A "person" does not have to be a human; a person is simply a being who has, or is worthy of, rights, such as the right to life or respect. So why should humans, Asgardian gods, and the Kree be considered persons, whereas androids, zombies, and animals are not? Perhaps the former have souls and the latter do not. That answer, however, begs the question of the nature of souls. How do we really know what a soul is and who has one?

It appears illegitimate to deny androids the ability to love based simply on the fact that they are inorganic and artificially developed. In arguing for animal rights, contemporary philosopher Peter Singer argues that different forms of prejudice, such as sexism and racism, involve members valuing their own group based on an arbitrary characteristic that other groups lack. *Speciesism*, according to Singer, is a prejudice or attitude of bias against members of other species.[20] A related prejudice may be at work in concluding that androids cannot love simply because they are artificial.

Singer might point out that, like animals, androids suffer and have interests. Beyond that, they can even acknowledge that they are marginalized in society. Obviously the Vision is interested in fighting evil; otherwise he would not engage in superhero activities. He also regularly displays both emotional and physical suffering.[21] Lastly, he acknowledges how, as an android, he is marginalized by others, remarking that "even among mutants, monsters, and man-gods, we artificial life-forms are still the least accepted."[22] Following Singer, then, we should refrain from *organicism*, the prejudice against synthetic creatures. Indeed, we should recognize that they have the same rights and privileges that we have, including the right to love and get married.

Love: American Style

While personhood may make androids morally "eligible" for love and loving, we still haven't answered the question of whether they *can* love. To do that, we have to ask what love really *is*. For our purposes, it is enough to say that love is a *concept*.

The American philosopher Charles S. Peirce (1839–1914) gave us the *pragmatic maxim*, which articulates a way to think of concepts and their meanings. Peirce instructs us as follows:

> Consider what effects, which might conceivably have practical bearings, we conceive the object of our conception to have. Then, our conception of these effects is the whole of our conception of the object.[23]

So when we consider a concept such as love, its meaning is the possible effects it has in the world we live in. If an android such as the Vision loved a human such as the Scarlet Witch, then how would his conception of love have any meaning or significance? The possible practical effects would include his caring for her, treating her with kindness, being receptive to her words, attending to her needs and feelings, and having a degree of physical intimacy with her. Clearly the Vision does all these things.

The pragmatic maxim isn't just a way of thinking about concepts; it also aids in clarifying our concepts. For example,

Baron Zemo might say he loves his pet dog Fritz. But if instead of providing and caring for him, Zemo neglects and abuses Fritz, then according to the pragmatic maxim, Zemo's love for his dog is meaningless, regardless of Zemo's vehement protests.

What if an android is programmed to give the illusion or appearance of love? Is "faking it" good enough? A human can also give the illusion of love. When the script calls for it, actors are trained to "program" themselves to act and respond as if they are in love. Obviously this looks like love, but it is not real since the actor does not *internally* feel the love. Similarly, an android or a human might state that they feel that they are in love, which is itself another practical effect of love, but the only way to tell whether they are in love is by their actions, how they conduct themselves, and their own testimony about their feelings, which is observable and testable. In a way, the real test is whether love is *felt* by each party.

So, despite the skepticism of some of the Avengers, an android and a human can love each other in a meaningful sense. The proof is not identifying what type of beings they are—whether an android is a person, for instance—but observing what their actions, feelings, conduct, and thoughts are.

NOTES

1. See Plato, *Symposium*, 199c–212b (in any reputable translation with the standard pagination), and Aristotle, *Nicomachean Ethics*, book VIII, chapters 1–8.

2. C. S. Lewis, *The Four Loves* (New York: Harcourt, Brace, 1960).

3. Ibid., 33.

4. Ibid., 30.

5. Ibid., 33.

6. Ibid.

7. Ibid., 70.

8. They first met in *Avengers*, vol. 1, #76 (May 1970), and reconciled their feelings for each other in #108 (February 1973), reprinted in *Essential Avengers Vol. 4* (2005) and *Vol. 5* (2006), respectively.

9. Lewis, *Four Loves*, 96.

10. Ibid., 99.

11. *Avengers*, vol. 1, #109 (March, 1973), reprinted in *Essential Avengers Vol. 5*.

12. Lewis, *Four Loves*, p. 131.

13. Ibid., 133.

14. Ibid., 135 (emphasis mine).

15. Ibid., 91.

16. Ibid., 137.

17. Ibid., 177.

18. Ibid., 178.

19. Quicksilver in *Avengers*, vol. 1, #110 (April 1973), reprinted in *Essential Avengers Vol. 5*.

20. See Peter Singer, "All Animals Are Equal," in *Applied Ethics*, ed. Peter Singer (New York: Oxford University Press, 1986), 215–228.

21. The Vision experienced overwhelming emotions and cried when he was welcomed into the Avengers in *Avengers*, vol. 1, #58 (November 1968), reprinted in *Essential Avengers Vol. 3* (2001). He also experienced painful incapacitating seizures in *Marvel Team-Up*, vol. 1, #5 (November 1972), reprinted in *Essential Marvel Team-Up Vol. 1* (2002).

22. He stated this to Machine Man, another artificial life form, in *Marvel Super-Hero Contest of Champions* #1 (June 1982), reprinted in *Avengers: The Contest* (2010).

23. Charles S. Peirce, "How to Make Our Ideas Clear," in *The Essential Peirce: Selected Philosophical Writings, vol. 1, 1867–1892*, ed. Nathan Houser and Christian Kloesel (Bloomington: Indiana University Press, 1992), 124–141, at 132.

THE WAY OF THE ARROW: HAWKEYE MEETS THE TAOIST MASTERS

Mark D. White

Though he has gone by several other names throughout his superhero career, such as Goliath and Ronin, Clint Barton will always be best known as Hawkeye, the Avenging Archer. Orphaned at a young age, Clint joined a traveling carnival with his older brother Barney and was trained in archery by Trick Shot, a member of the troupe and a part-time criminal to boot. After being shown up by Iron Man, Clint sought glory as the masked adventurer Hawkeye, only to be confused for a criminal himself. Soon he met Natasha Romanova, the Russian spy known as the Black Widow who was bent on destroying Tony Stark (before becoming a hero herself). Clint fell for her and embraced her life of crime. After the Russian government retaliated against the Widow for trying to defect, however, Clint vowed to make amends for his past, starting with applying for membership in the Avengers.[1] Along with the Scarlet Witch and Quicksilver, who had also found themselves on the wrong side of the law early in their careers, Clint completed the second lineup of the Avengers that would forever be known as "Cap's Kooky Quartet."[2]

The rest is comics history, albeit a fairly convoluted history involving several deaths and resurrections, as well as joining the Avengers, the Defenders, the West Coast Avengers, the Great Lakes Avengers(!), the Thunderbolts, the New Avengers, and the Secret Avengers. And of course there were relationships with many women, including Black Widow and Mockingbird (Bobbi Morse), the latter of whom he married after their first case together.[3] His fellow Avengers think of Clint as brash and cocky, but his demeanor masks profound self-doubt, stemming from his unlucky childhood, his early mistakes in the costume, and comparisons with the noblest (Captain America), strongest (Thor), and smartest (Iron Man, Hank Pym) heroes in the Marvel Universe. Clint's perpetual underdog status, whether deserved or not, brings to mind the Eastern philosophy of Taoism, several elements of which we'll explore in this chapter.

Don't Try So Hard, Clint

The most famous work in Taoist (pronounced "dow-ist") philosophy is the *Tao Te Ching*, which is often translated as "The Way of Life." Said to have been written by Lao Tzu (pronounced "loud-suh") around 500 BCE—give or take a century—it prescribes a way of living for ordinary people as well as tips for sound governance by those in positions of authority.[4] But if good living is understood to involve self-governance, the entire *Tao Te Ching* can be read as a guide to aligning oneself with the ways of nature rather than fighting them.

Experience Wise [handwritten annotation]

One of the clearest—yet most paradoxical—examples of this respect for the ways of nature is the concept of *wei wu wei* (pronounced "way woo way"), or action through inaction: "do nondoing, strive for nonstriving."[5] Rather than implying passivity or laziness, *wei wu wei* recommends aligning yourself with the natural harmony of the universe and acknowledging your limited ability to alter it (as well as the folly in trying to). Effort should not be wasted on things that cannot be changed, but preserved for things that can, and wisdom lies in knowing which is which. In this sense, *wei wu wei* is very similar in spirit to the serenity prayer of theologian Reinhold Niebuhr (1892–1971), the most popular phrasing of which is, "God grant me the serenity to accept the things I cannot change; courage to change the things I can change; and wisdom to know the difference."[6]

To be sure, no one would confuse Trick Shot for a Taoist sage or wise man—he is a drunken, loutish, two-bit thief—but he does know his archery, and he gives Hawkeye a run for his money many times throughout his career. When Trick Shot trains a young Clint Barton, he tells him, "You must learn to use your bow gently, naturally, instinctively! Such is the way of the arrow!"[7] To use a bow and arrow is to harness nature at its most basic, and the successful archer must work with the bow, not against it. As Hawkeye thinks to himself at one point, to make a successful shot you must "be in the now," one with the bow, your surroundings, and yourself—in short, one with nature.[8]

Hawkeye's effortless skill with the bow and arrow certainly illustrates *wei wu wei*, but it must be remembered that it took much hard work to develop his amazing skills. Unfortunately, he wields those skills with arrogance and brashness, a demeanor that doesn't always sit well with his fellow Avengers—especially Captain America. As Lao Tzu wrote of sages, "Not congratulating themselves, they are therefore meritorious," and "Those who glorify themselves have no merit, those who are proud of themselves do not last."[9] By bragging of his abilities and heroism, Hawkeye detracts from them; he calls attention to his deeds instead of letting them speak for themselves, which violates the spirit of *wei wu wei*.

You'd think Clint would have learned this lesson given his origins, trying to one-up Iron Man and instead being mistaken for a criminal. Lao Tzu wrote that if people "do not dwell on success, then by this very nondwelling success will not leave."[10] In the beginning, Clint tried too hard to be famous. It backfired, and he risked becoming infamous instead. He needed to learn that the best way to achieve fame is to *not* seek it. After all, he was never more famous than he was as an Avenger, where he used his skills as an archer to fight crime and villainy rather than to win acclaim. Lao Tzu would hardly recommend a life chasing fame, but if Clint wants to do it, then *wei wu wei* can show him how—by *not* doing it.

When Is a Butcher Like an Archer?

Whereas Lao Tzu wrote the *Tao Te Ching* in the form of poetry or verse, Chuang Tzu, a Taoist scholar from the fourth century BCE who built upon Lao Tzu's ideas, used prose to tell stories or parables that illustrated his Taoist ideas. It is appropriate that Clint Barton's father was a butcher, a trade that demands skill and focus much like archery does—and happens to have been the subject of one of Chuang Tzu's tales. In it, a king admires a butcher's skill at carving an ox, and asks him how he does it so effortlessly yet so well:

> When I first began to cut up oxen, all I saw was an ox. . . . Now I meet it with spirit rather than look at it with my eyes. When sensory knowledge stops, then the spirit is ready to act. . . . The joints have spaces in between, whereas the edge of the cleaver blade has no thickness. When that which has no thickness is put into

that which has no space, there is ample room for moving the blade. This is why the edge of my cleaver is still as sharp as if it had newly come from the whetstone.[11]

 After hearing this, the king says, "Excellent! Having heard the word of a butcher, I have found the way to nurture life."[12]

We can easily imagine someone being impressed in the same way by Hawkeye's skill with a bow and arrow, especially how it respects the harmony of nature and the conservation of effort. Chuang Tzu's parable can be considered a refinement of *wei wu wei*, emphasizing that the path of least resistance—the space between the joints, for instance—is the natural one to travel to ensure success in life. Hawkeye can make shots that seem impossible to us, and that amaze even his fellow Avengers, but he's not going to seek out the most difficult shot in an emergency. He may do it in practice to test himself, or to show off at an exhibition (or to a woman), but in the midst of battle he is going to take the shot with the best chance of success, which even for an experienced archer will be the most straightforward one possible. In other words, there is a time to see how good you are by testing your limits, and a time to show how good you are by getting the job done, and for the most part Hawkeye finds that balance.[13]

In an early Avengers tale, Hawkeye prepares to fire electromagnetic arrows to rein in the Black Panther's runaway airship. When the Panther says, "Heaven help us if you miss," Hawkeye replies, "Bite your tongue, mister! I never miss . . . Just settle back and relax, little buddies." But when his bowstring breaks and the Vision has to save the day, Clint is devastated: "One crummy broken string . . . and I'm Mister Fifth Wheel! I'm not in you guys' league." After the Avengers find out that Black Widow is in trouble, they rush off without Clint, who is judged to be too personally involved. Clint agrees, but for a different reason, saying to himself, "They were right, blast 'em! A hothead like me might just foul up things . . . get the whole bunch of us killed!" So he decides to take Hank Pym's growth serum and become the new Goliath to rescue Natasha. When the couple returns to Avengers Mansion, Clint confirms his intentions to leave his "weak" Hawkeye persona behind by snapping his bow in half.[14]

Ironically, it is during the massive intergalactic conflict known as the Kree-Skrull War that Clint realizes his true nature is to be an archer, not a chemically enhanced giant.[15] Nearly out of Pym's growth serum and finding himself on a Skrull warship on a destructive mission to Earth, he fashions a bow and arrow from materials he finds on the ship and uses them to destroy the ship, narrowly escaping with his life.[16] Earlier, he thought he was failing his fellow Avengers with his archery skills, and tried to be a giant strongman instead (ironically, another carnival identity). But by denying his true nature and not making use of what he did best, he was not following the path of *wei wu wei*; instead, he was trying too hard to be something that he was not.

Hawkeye, Humble?

His brief time as Goliath shows that Clint feels a tremendous need to live up to the example of his peers and earn their acceptance as well as his own. In fact, he leaves the team altogether soon thereafter, saying that he's "had my fill of being poor old Hawkeye, the stupid Avenger" (ironically, after having his archery prowess praised by none other than Thor).[17] Clint Barton has many admirable qualities, including not just his tremendous skill with the bow and arrow and his fantastic athleticism but his heroic nature as well. However, he lacks one quality that is particularly emphasized by the Taoist masters: humility. He is often described as brash and cocky by friends and foes alike, but this behavior masks deep-rooted insecurities; as Natasha once noted, Clint is "so full of conceit and insecurity at the same time."[18] As his words show, he suffers from feelings of inadequacy compared with his mightier colleagues in the Avengers—none more than his friend, mentor, and sparring partner, Captain America.

From the moment he joins the Avengers, Clint challenges Cap's authority, accusing him of being a washed-up "square" and a World War II relic. Their conflict comes to a head in their fourth issue together, when Hawkeye sticks his finger in Cap's face—an image reproduced time and again in future stories—accusing him of poor leadership and trying to "push your weight around all the time."[19] But as their relationship develops, Clint gains tremendous respect for the Sentinel of Liberty, coming to admire his wise and measured leadership, especially when Clint heads his own team, the West Coast Avengers. Soon after he puts together the charter lineup, a stranger appears in their new headquarters, and Clint thinks to himself, "Should I let the others catch our intruder . . . or rush in and collar him myself? How would Cap handle this?"[20] Soon afterward, Clint gets into a petty battle with Iron Man after discovering that the man wearing the armor wasn't Tony Stark but his successor James Rhodes. Clint accuses him of being "an amateur Iron Man," while Rhodey defends his short but successful tenure as the Armored Avenger. This leads Clint to recall his insolence with Cap in the early days of the Avengers and to "wonder how Cap put up with me?"[21]

Consistent with his origins, Clint wants to be highly regarded by his peers, but he needs to learn the lessons of the Taoists—especially since Cap follows the same wisdom, particularly regarding humility and leadership. We've already mentioned Hawkeye's glory seeking, which Cap doesn't engage in; he shuns the spotlight as well as the praise that it brings. When leading the Avengers, Cap prefers to boost others rather than himself. As Lao Tzu wrote with respect to effective leadership, "When sages wish to rise above people, they lower themselves to them in their speech. When they want to precede people, they go after them in status."[22] Cap often finds himself giving pep speeches to his self-doubting teammate, early on telling him, "You have a lot of potential, Avenger. More than the rest. That's why I'm pushing you. You could be the best we've ever had."[23] Much later, when Hawkeye marvels at Cap's skill with his shield and asked how he does it, Cap simply says, "Practice and passion, Clint. Just like you."[24] When Hawkeye continues to challenge Cap's leadership, even after decades together, Cap still deflects the criticism, offering Clint the spot if he thinks he can do it better, and reassuring his old friend, "You're a good man, Clint."[25] Rather than take the chance to gloat about his own skills as a hero or leader, Cap chooses to praise Clint, raising him in status while giving him incentive to be even better: "You really are the best of us, but only when you want to be."[26]

Humility can have strategic benefit as well, especially when it comes to fooling your enemies. When Crossfire captures Hawkeye, planning to kill him and use his dead body to draw out the rest of Earth's heroes, he tells Clint he chose him because he is "the weakest, most vulnerable known costumed crime fighter in town."[27] But as you can easily guess, Crossfire grossly underestimates our favorite archer, who escapes his trap by outsmarting the villain, who then tries to kill Clint with his own bow and arrow but ironically discovers he is not strong enough to pull the string. As Lao Tzu wrote, "No calamity is greater than underestimating opponents," which also implies an advantage to appearing weak to your enemies, as Clint learns (but, it seems, has not taken to heart).[28]

The Life and Death of a Hero

Like so many heroes in the Marvel Universe, Hawkeye has had firsthand experience with death, and lived (again) to tell about it—both times. When a mentally unstable Scarlet Witch attacks Avengers Mansion with a Kree armada that she fabricates with her reality-altering powers, Clint is shot in the back by a number of Kree soldiers. Refusing to die that way, he grabs a nearby Kree, activates his jetpack, and flies into the Kree warship, destroying it and killing himself.[29] We could choose to see this simply as one final grandstanding move from the former carnival showman, but instead we will use it to explore two final themes in Taoism, heroism and death, both of which involve (in the spirit of *wei wu wei*) sacrifice "without sacrifice."

As Lao Tzu wrote, "Sages put themselves last, and they were first; they excluded themselves, and they survived."[30] This is true of heroes as well: by putting their own needs and safety aside to protect others, they ensure their own survival, either literally (continuing as heroes if they live) or metaphorically (as legacies after their death). Hawkeye makes the ultimate sacrifice when he flies into the Kree warship, which ensures that he will be remembered as a hero for years to come. And after Kate Bishop, one of the Young Avengers and a fine archer, stands up to Captain America like only Clint has before her, he bestows on her the name Hawkeye (as well as his equipment).[31] Hawkeye is now a legacy, a mantle to be passed on to future heroes.[32]

Lao Tzu asked, "If people usually don't fear death, how can death be used to scare them?"[33] Through his heroism, Clint Barton has proven that he does not fear death—and even if he did, he doesn't let that fear prevent him from being a hero. Lao Tzu also wrote (in one of his more straightforward moments), "Sages always consider it good to save people," and in this sense, even Hawkeye is a sage. It isn't just about superheroics and Avenging for Clint, though, at least later in his career. When he recently took a road trip to Myrtle Beach, he stopped to help stranded motorists along the way (granted, female stranded motorists). He ended up saving a stripper from a lout in a bar, an act that embroiled him in a scheme involving war crimes in Laos and a stolen religious relic—and he didn't put on his costume until the end of the six-issue story line.[34]

Soon after Hawkeye's death, the Scarlet Witch (under the sway of her brother Quicksilver) uses her mutant powers to re-form the entire world into one dominated by mutants under the rule of her father, Magneto. She also resurrects Hawkeye, to whom she had long been close, but after he threatens her life she "disassembles" him again. He is believed dead, but a mysterious copy of his newspaper obituary pinned to a wall with an arrow leads us (and the Avengers) to suspect otherwise.[35] After seeking out (and, we might say, "reconciling with") the Scarlet Witch, who apparently has no memory of the destruction she caused, Clint adopts the identity of Ronin until returning to the classic Hawkeye colors after the Siege of Asgard ends and the "Heroic Age" begins.[36]

The unique nature of Hawkeye's experiences during this second period recalls one of Chuang Tzu's most famous tales:

> Once Chuang Chou dreamed he was a butterfly. He was happy as a butterfly, enjoying himself and going where he wanted. He did not know he was Chou. Suddenly he awoke, whereupon he was startled to find he was Chou. He didn't know whether Chou had dreamed he was a butterfly, or if a butterfly were dreaming it was Chou.[37]

Earlier in the same chapter of his works, Chuang Tzu connects this idea with death: "How do I know the dead do not regret having longed for life at first?"[38] He's making two points here: first, that there is no way to compare two such different states of being to determine which one is more "real," as in the butterfly or Chou. The Scarlet Witch completely altered reality to fit Quicksilver's conception of the perfect world: who's to say which was more real, that reality or the original one? Second, there is also no way to say which one you would prefer: is it better to be the butterfly or Chou, and is it better to be alive or dead? To the Taoist, life and death are both parts of nature. Neither is to be celebrated more than the other, but both are to be welcomed as part of the *tao* ("the Way"). Clint has been both, and in two different realities—if only we could ask him which he preferred!

The Way of the Archer

After Clint took up the Hawkeye identity most recently, he thought to himself, "Been a while, but here, now, feeling the pull of the string, the fletching of the arrow between my fingers, the weight of the quiver on my back . . . it's like coming home."[39] He has returned to his true path, the one that expresses *wei wu wei* in that it is the most natural and effortless one for him. It is only natural, then, to end this chapter with a final quote from Lao Tzu: "The Way of Heaven is like drawing a bow; the high is lowered, the low is raised; excess is reduced, need is fulfilled."[40] The Way moderates all things and keeps them in balance, and after all his experiences with love, loss, and struggle, Clint Barton may be on his way to realizing the Way as well.

NOTES

1. *Tales of Suspense* #57, 60, and 64 (1964–1965), reprinted in *Essential Iron Man Vol. 1* (2002), and *Avengers*, vol. 1, #16 (May 1965), reprinted in *Essential Avengers Vol. 1* (1998). For a slightly updated version of his introduction to the Avengers, see *Hawkeye: Blindspot* #2 (May 2011), reprinted in *Hawkeye: Blindspot* (2011).

2. For more on the themes of redemption and rehabilitation, see the chapters titled "Forgivers Assemble?" by Daniel P. Malloy and "Cap's Kooky Quartet: Is Rehabilitation Possible?" by Andrew Terjesen in this volume.

3. *Hawkeye*, vol. 1, #4 (December 1983), reprinted in the hardcover collection *Avengers: Hawkeye* (2009).

4. Many scholars now think the *Tao Te Ching* is more likely an anonymous collection of accumulated wisdom than the work of a single man, but for the sake of convenience we will refer to Lao Tzu when discussing it.

5. *Tao Te Ching*, chapter 63. Unless noted otherwise, all translations of Taoist texts are by Thomas Cleary and can be found in *The Taoist Classics*, vol. 1 (Boston: Shambhala Publications, 1994).

6. This concept is also found in the writings of the Stoic philosopher Epictetus (55–135); see Book 4, chapter 4 of his *Discourses*.

7. *Solo Avengers* #2 (January 1988), reprinted in *Avengers: Solo Avengers Classic Vol. 1* (2012).

8. *Hawkeye & Mockingbird* #3 (October 2010), reprinted in *Hawkeye & Mockingbird: Ghosts* (2011), which contains all six issues of the short-lived series. This advice comes in handy when Clint has to fight his brother and Baron Zemo after being blinded (*Hawkeye: Blindspot* #4, July 2011).

9. *Tao Te Ching*, chapters 22 and 24.

10. *Tao Te Ching*, chapter 2.

11. *Chuang Tzu*, chapter 3, 66–67, in *The Taoist Classics*.

12. Ibid.

13. However, in *Avengers*, vol. 3, #79 (April 2004), reprinted in *Avengers Vol. 4: Lionheart of Avalon* (2004), Hawkeye tries to take on the entire Wrecking Crew, a trio of power-houses who have given Thor a run for his money. After he is brutally beaten down, Clint confesses to the Wasp that he did it for her after seeing her ex-husband Hank Pym (who once beat her) manhandle her (*Avengers*, vol. 3, #82, July 2004, reprinted in *Avengers Vol. 5: Once an Invader*, 2004).

14. *Avengers*, vol. 1, #63–64 (April–May 1969), reprinted in *Essential Avengers Vol. 3* (2001).

15. *Avengers: Kree-Skrull War* (2008), reprinting *Avengers*, vol. 1, #89–97 (June 1971–March 1972), also reprinted (in black and white) in *Essential Avengers Vol. 4* (2005). For more on the Kree-Skrull War, see the chapter titled "Fighting the Good Fight: Military Ethics and the Kree-Skrull War" by Christopher Robichaud in this volume.

16. *Avengers*, vol. 1, #99 (May 1972), reprinted in *Essential Avengers Vol. 5* (2006).

17. *Avengers*, vol. 1, #109 (March 1973), reprinted in *Essential Avengers Vol. 5*.

18. *Thunderbolts* #43 (October 2000), reprinted in *Avengers Assemble Vol. 3* (2006).

19. *Avengers*, vol. 1, #20 (September 1965), reprinted in *Essential Avengers Vol. 1*. Some things never change: Clint even picks a fight with Steve Rogers's successor, Bucky Barnes, over who "should have" taken over the mantle of Captain America after Rogers's death (*New Avengers: The Reunion* #1, May 2009, reprinted in *New Avengers: The Reunion*, 2010). (Tony Stark offered Clint the title in *Fallen Son: The Death of Captain America* #3, July 2007, reprinted in *Fallen Son: The Death of Captain America*, 2008.)

20. *West Coast Avengers*, vol. 1, #1 (September 1984), reprinted in *Avengers: West Coast Avengers Assemble* (2010).

21. *West Coast Avengers*, vol. 1, #4 (December 1984), reprinted in *Avengers: West Coast Avengers Assemble*.

22. *Tao Te Ching*, chapter 66.

23. See the flashback scene in *Hawkeye: Blindspot* #2 (May 2011). For a textbook example of tough love from Cap when Clint is particularly down on himself, see *Hawkeye & Mockingbird* #6 (January 2011).

24. *Avengers*, vol. 3, #75 (February 2004), reprinted in *Avengers: The Search for She-Hulk* (2010).

25. *Avengers*, vol. 3, #6 (July 1998), reprinted in *Avengers Assemble Vol. 1* (2004).

26. *Hawkeye: Blindspot* #2. For more on Captain America's modesty, see my chapter "Captain America and the Virtue of Modesty" in *Superheroes: The Best of Philosophy and Pop Culture*, ed. William Irwin (Hoboken, NJ: John Wiley & Sons, 2011).

27. *Hawkeye*, vol. 1, #4.

28. *Tao Te Ching*, chapter 69. This is similar to the teachings of Sun Tzu in *The Art of War*, considered to be a Taoist classic in its own right.

29. *Avengers*, vol. 3, #502 (November 2004), reprinted in *Avengers Disassembled* (2005).

30. *Tao Te Ching*, chapter 7.

31. *Young Avengers* #12 (August 2006), reprinted in *Young Avengers: Family Matters* (2007).

32. For more on superhero mantles, see the chapter by Stephen Nelson titled "Superhero Identity: Case Studies in the Avengers" in this volume.

33. *Tao Te Ching*, chapter 74.

34. *Hawkeye*, vol. 3, #1–6 (December 2003–May 2004).

35. *House of M* (2006).

36. Clint finds the Scarlet Witch in *New Avengers*, vol. 1, #26 (January 2007), appears (unidentified) as Ronin in issue #27 (April 2007), and is shown (in flashback) assuming the Ronin identity in #30 (July 2007), all reprinted in *New Avengers Vol. 6: Revolution* (2007). He becomes Hawkeye once more in *Enter the Heroic Age* (July 2010), reprinted in *Hawkeye & Mockingbird: Ghosts* (2011).

37. Chuang Tzu, chapter 2, 65, in *The Taoist Classics*. A similar argument was put forward by philosopher René Descartes (1596–1650) to question our knowledge of reality; see his *Meditations on First Philosophy* (1641), Meditation 1. And it's not too much of a stretch to extend this to the Skrull who impersonated Mockingbird for so many years! (For Mockingbird's side of the story, see *New Avengers: The Reunion*.)

38. Ibid., 64.

39. *Hawkeye & Mockingbird* #1 (August 2010).

40. *Tao Te Ching*, chapter 77.

APPENDIX

Why Are There Four Volumes of *Avengers*?

Since there are so many *Avengers* titles, which seem to be relaunched or renumbered as often as Iron Man updates his armor, here is a "simple" guide to delving into the Avengers canon, covering the main ongoing titles (and by necessity leaving out many miniseries and one-shots).

The first volume of *Avengers* started in September 1963 and lasted for over four hundred issues (and annuals) until September 1996. In 1984, the *West Coast Avengers* appeared in a self-titled miniseries (an obvious ploy to get Hawkeye out of Avengers Mansion), followed in 1985 by an ongoing series that lasted until 1994 (after changing its title to *Avengers West Coast* in 1989). In order to keep busy, Hawkeye also headlined the *Solo Avengers* title (which featured another Avenger in the backup story) starting in 1987 and lasting until 1991 (also changing its title to *Avengers Spotlight* in 1989).

The first *Avengers* run ended when the Avengers were "Heroes Reborn," thrown into a pocket dimension of distorted anatomy and even worse costume design. The second volume of *Avengers* mercifully lasted only thirteen issues (from November 1996 to November 1997). You will notice that this run is never cited in this book—for a reason. ('Nuff said.) The third volume of *Avengers* started in February 1998 when our heroes returned to the normal Marvel Universe with a near-classic lineup (and the Avengers spotlight now focused on the Scarlet Witch's navel). In September 2004, the series was renumbered starting with issue #500 to reflect the original volume's numbering (as if it had been followed throughout all the volumes). However, this was also the beginning of "Avengers Disassembled," as the team and mansion were decimated by a very angry Scarlet Witch. (You connect the dots, my friend.)

Then the fun started: after much soul-searching on the part of Iron Man and Captain America, the first volume of *New Avengers* launched in January 2005 (yes, the same month that the original Avengers disbanded *forever!*). It was followed by *Young Avengers* in April 2005, which lasted a year and told the story of a group of second-generation heroes (including another upstart archer). Then the *Civil War* happened in 2006, and the New Avengers reemerged afterward as an underground ragtag band of renegades fighting against superhero registration—and yes, Clint Barton was there. But the pro-registration forces, led by Iron Man, had their own team. The *Mighty Avengers* title started in May 2007, followed soon by *Avengers: The Initiative* in June 2007, detailing the training of young heroes (not including the Young Avengers, who continued on in a series of one-shots and miniseries).

After the Skrulls' *Secret Invasion* ended in January 2009, the lineups of the New and Mighty Avengers were shaken up (but the titles continued, without even renumbering them!). More important, *Dark Avengers* launched in March 2009, featuring evil doppelgängers for key Avengers like Hawkeye and Ms. Marvel, and led by none other than Norman Osborn. After Osborn's Siege of Asgard in summer 2010, all the Avengers titles—*New, Mighty, Dark,* and *Initiative*—ended. In the new *Heroic Age*, not only was a second volume of *New Avengers* launched, but we also saw a fourth volume of *Avengers* as the classic title was revived for the first time in fifteen years. Add to this *Secret Avengers* (Steve Rogers's black ops team, later headed by Hawkeye), *Avengers Academy* (the latest young-heroes-in-training title), and *Avengers Assemble*, which began in March 2012—not to mention the live-action movie, cunningly titled *Avengers*, and the animated TV show *The Avengers: Earth's Mightiest Heroes*—and the Avengers are truly Earth's mightiest comics, television, and film franchise.

CONTRIBUTORS

Avengers Academy

Adam Barkman has a PhD from the Free University of Amsterdam and is associate professor of philosophy at Redeemer University College in Ancaster, Ontario. He is the author of *C. S. Lewis and Philosophy as a Way of Life*, *Through Common Things*, and *Above All Things*, and is the coeditor of *Manga and Philosophy* and *The Philosophy of Ang Lee*. However, to his kids, Heather (Waspie-Turtle) and Tristan (Hulk-Puppy), he is simply known as Thor-Lion, and this is their song: "Avengers: Assemble! Always, we will fight as one, the battle boo-boo-boo . . ."

Arno Bogaerts is currently finishing his studies in philosophy and ethics at the Vrije Universiteit Brussel in Belgium, where he has written several essays focusing on the superhero and its genre. He also writes for the Belgian comic book site Brainfreeze and will contribute a chapter to the upcoming *Superman and Philosophy*. Convinced that Belgian beer can easily beat the best mead Asgard has to offer, he and his buddies plan to challenge both Thor and Tony Stark to a local drinking contest.

Roy T. Cook is associate professor of philosophy at the University of Minnesota–Twin Cities, a resident fellow at the Minnesota Center for Philosophy of Science, and an associate fellow at the Northern Institute of Philosophy–University of Aberdeen, Scotland. He is the author of *A Dictionary of Philosophical Logic*, editor of *The Arché Papers on the Mathematics of Abstraction*, and has published numerous academic articles on paradoxes, the philosophy of logic, the philosophy of mathematics, and, more recently, the aesthetics of comics. He is also coeditor (with Aaron Meskin) of *The Art of Comics: A Philosophical Approach*. Despite the best efforts of artists and writers, his early romance with Jennifer Walters was censored by the Comics Code Authority, and as a result the steamy details will forever remain a secret.

Sarah K. Donovan is an associate professor in the Department of Philosophy and Religious Studies at Wagner College in New York City. Her teaching and research interests include feminist, social, moral, and Continental philosophy, and she has coauthored articles for books in the present series on Batman, *Watchmen*, Iron Man, and Green Lantern. While performing research with the Dark Avengers, she became friends with Lindy Reynolds, but now feels guilty about assuring her that helicopter rides are completely safe.

Andrew Zimmerman Jones is the physics guide at About. com and author of *String Theory for Dummies*. He lives in central Indiana with his wife and two young sons, occasionally writing essays in august collections such as *Heroes and Philosophy* and *Green Lantern and Philosophy*. In his spare time, he searches for Jones Particles, theoretical particles that will shrink your waistline.

Charles Klayman is a term instructor of philosophy at John A. Logan College in Carterville, Illinois. Since Xavier's Institute for Higher Learning rejected his application, he is completing his doctoral studies at Southern Illinois University Carbondale. His research interests include classical American philosophy and aesthetics. Despite possessing the ability to befuddle minds, he was denied Avengers membership; apparently, carrying a thick philosophy book is not the same as carrying a mystical hammer or an indestructible shield.

Daniel P. Malloy quit the Avengers in protest after the Scarlet Witch married the Vision, maintaining (against Klayman's chapter) that walking toasters don't have the right to marry. There was also a slight dispute with Jarvis, which has since been settled out of court. Since then, Daniel has spent his time as a lecturer in philosophy at Appalachian State University, teaching introductory courses and writing about the intersections between philosophy and popular culture.

Louis P. Melançon dresses like Captain America and asks for super-soldier serum at every medical appointment he has. So far it's only resulted in flu and anthrax vaccinations. While he has no experience (yet) in fighting the Skrulls, Kree, or any time-traveling villains bent on world domination, as a U.S. Army officer Louis has had a wide variety of tactical and strategic combat arms and intelligence experience. He has been awarded the Bronze Star Medal and holds master's degrees from the Joint Military Intelligence College (now National Intelligence University) and King's College, London. His greatest achievement, however, is teaching his two-year-old daughter to identify all the Pet Avengers by name.

Stephen M. Nelson is a PhD candidate in the Department of Philosophy at the University of Minnesota. He teaches courses in a variety of areas, and his research centers on the philosophy of language, philosophy of logic, and metaphysics. Being a direct descendant of Odin through his Icelandic side (which he can prove with detailed genealogical records), Stephen has always felt a distinct—almost brotherly—bond with Thor, and, by extension, the ragtag band of superheroes Thor runs with.

Robert Powell—or "Troy" when he's under the influence of a special top-secret serum—is a master's candidate in the Conflict Analysis and Management Program at Royal Roads University in Victoria, British Columbia, with an undergraduate background in psychology and philosophy. Troy is also a research analyst with the Sentinel Project for Genocide Prevention, a Toronto-based NGO, working on an open source early warning system for genocide—or what Troy likes to think of as the "Cerebro of ethnic conflict." What fewer people know is that Troy is secretly working on an upgrade to the serum that created the Sentry, believing we all must learn to rein in our darker natures before we can rise and shine as heroes of the world in our own domains.

Nicholas Richardson is an associate professor in the Department of Physical Sciences at Wagner College in New York City, where he teaches general, advanced inorganic, and medicinal chemistry. He has coauthored articles for books in the present series on Batman, *Watchmen*, Iron Man, and Green Lantern. He was initially asked by Norman Osborn to join the Dark Avengers, but somehow the paperwork got lost, and Osborn had to step in at the last minute to become the Iron Patriot himself.

Christopher Robichaud is a lecturer in ethics and public policy at the Harvard Kennedy School of Government. The Avengers often consult him on matters of moral and political philosophy. Well, Nick Fury forces them to. Captain America politely listens. Iron Man totally ignores him. Black Widow threatens to kill him if he doesn't shut up. Hawkeye echoes that sentiment. Thor simply laughs and invites him out for a beer. And Hulk, mercifully, never shows up.

Jason Southworth is an adjunct professor of philosophy at Fort Hays State University in Hays, Kansas. He has written chapters for many Philosophy and Pop Culture volumes, including ones on *Inception*, X-Men, and Final Fantasy. He is curious about the application process for the Pet Avengers; if Miss Lion is a member, surely it was a mistake not to invite Hepzibah, the fierce defender of the Southworth-Tallman household.

Tony Spanakos was never invited to join the Avengers despite being recognized by his wife, friends, and students as "positively inhuman." Having emerged from the Terrigen Mists with no useful power other than the ability to read dry texts comfortably on a crowded subway car, he has pursued scholarship for several years, teaching politics at Montclair State University in New Jersey and New York University. He published a number of articles on political economy and democratization in Latin America before being called to join the Defenders. While holding out for an Avengers gig (if Hank Pym can do it, why not him?), he has written essays for *Batman and Philosophy*, *Watchmen and Philosophy*, *Iron Man and Philosophy*, and the forthcoming *Spider-Man and Philosophy*.

Ruth Tallman is an assistant professor of philosophy at Barry University in Miami Shores, Florida. She has written chapters for other popular philosophy volumes on Sherlock Holmes, the Rolling Stones, and Christmas. She's not wild about the relationship between Tigra and Hank Pym because it sends the wrong message to impressionable young cats like Hepzibah, the fearless protector of the Southworth-Tallman household.

Andrew Terjesen earned his PhD in philosophy from Duke University and taught for a number of years at Austin College, Washington and Lee University, and Rhodes College. His philosophical interests include moral psychology, early modern philosophy, and the philosophy of law. He also enjoys writing about the intersections of philosophy and pop culture with essays in this series about the X-Men, *Watchmen*, Iron Man, Green Lantern, Spider-Man, and Superman. Andrew has recently enrolled in law school, but was disappointed that his criminal law professor did not cover the issue of transtemporal jurisdiction in the landmark case of *Kang v. Immortus v. Scarlet Centurion v. Rama Tut*. (Andrew suspects that the professor is a Skrull.)

Mark D. White is the chair of the Department of Political Science, Economics, and Philosophy at the College of Staten Island/CUNY, where he teaches courses that combine economics, philosophy, and law. He is the author of *Kantian Ethics and Economics: Autonomy, Dignity, and Character* (Stanford, 2011), and has edited (or coedited) books for the present series on Batman, *Watchmen*, Iron Man, Green Lantern, and Superman. If he had the Scarlet Witch's ability to alter reality, he'd make sure he got to edit this book too.

INDEX

From Jarvis's Secret Files